The under-estimation of urban poverty in low- and middle-income nations

David Satterthwaite

Working Paper on Poverty Reduction in Urban Areas 14

This document is an output from a project funded by the UK Department for International Development (DFID) for the benefit of developing countries and by the Swedish International Development Cooperation Agency (Sida). For DFID, this was under a research contract for "Seeking more accurate and inclusive measures of urban poverty" (contract No: 8131). The views expressed are not necessarily those of the DFID or Sida.

This is one of two papers looking at how poverty is defined and measured; the other paper is *Understanding urban poverty; what the Poverty Reduction Strategy Papers tell us* by Diana Mitlin and, like this one, is available as a published working paper from www.earthprint.org or electronically at www.iied.org/urban/downloads.html. In addition to these two papers, there are a series of working papers on poverty reduction in urban areas that are also available in print or electronically; a full list of these is given at the end of this paper.

ABOUT THE AUTHOR

David Satterthwaite is a Senior Fellow at the International Institute for Environment and Development (IIED) and also on the teaching staff of the London School of Economics and of University College London. He has been editor of the international journal *Environment and Urbanization* from its inception in 1989. He is also a member of the Millennium Taskforce on Improving the Lives of Slum Dwellers and served on the US National Academy of Sciences Panel on Urban Population Dynamics (2001-2003) and on the Inter-Governmental Panel on Climate Change (2001-2003).

He has written or edited various books, including *Squatter Citizen* (with Jorge E. Hardoy), *The Earthscan Reader on Sustainable Cities, Environmental Problems in an Urbanizing World* (with Jorge E. Hardoy and Diana Mitlin) and *Empowering Squatter Citizen; Local Government, Civil Society and Urban Poverty Reduction* (with Diana Mitlin), which are published by Earthscan, London. In 2004, he was made an Honorary Professor at the University of Hull.

Address: Human Settlements Programme
IIED
3 Endsleigh Street
London WC1H ODD, UK

Tel: (44) 207 388 2117
Fax: (44) 207 388 2826
E-mail: David@iied.org

ISBN: 1 84369 513 8

CONTENTS

TABLES

FIGURE

ANNEXES

iv

Preface and acknowledgements

This paper suggests that the scale of urban poverty is under-stated in the official statistics used by governments and international agencies in most low- and middle-income nations and seeks to explain why this is so. Part of this explanation is the extent to which the general literature on the definition and measurement of poverty does not draw on available evidence on urban poverty, and this paper seeks to marshal enough of this evidence to demonstrate this. But the scale and nature of urban poverty are not well documented in many nations. This also means that those who work in urban areas see and work within extreme poverty, but find that most general texts suggest it is not serious or widespread. I cannot produce empirical evidence proving the very poor quality and overcrowded conditions, and lack of infrastructure and services that exist in all the tenements and informal settlements I have visited over the last 30 years, or of the health burdens, premature deaths, evictions and other difficulties that their inhabitants talk about. But spending time walking through Kibera or other informal settlements in Nairobi (which house around half the city's population) makes it difficult to accept suggestions that a very small proportion of Kenya's urban population is poor. Walking through informal settlements in Dar es Salaam and listening to the inhabitants discuss their difficulties with accessing water and sanitation makes it difficult to take seriously the official statistic that 98 percent of Tanzania's urban population have access to 'improved' sanitation. Sitting in on discussions by women pavement and slum dwellers in Mumbai about the difficulties they face getting water makes it difficult to accept the official statistic that 100 percent of the city's population has access to piped water. When statistics are being produced on urban poverty where data is lacking, perhaps there is a need to develop ways to test the validity of these statistics, drawing on those with knowledge of conditions in the urban areas in question.

This paper draws together and updates both published and unpublished work that I have undertaken over the last ten years on this topic. The issues discussed in this paper were raised in Satterthwaite 1995 and Satterthwaite 1997a, and discussed in more detail in Jonsson and Satterthwaite 2000 (an unpublished background paper prepared for the US National Research Council's Panel on Urban Population Dynamics, whose report *Cities Transformed* was published in 2003 – see Montgomery, Stren, Cohen and Reed 2003) and Mitlin and Satterthwaite 2001. Support from the UK Department for International Development (DFID) allowed it to be developed further, during 2003 and 2004. Diana Mitlin has written a companion paper to this, entitled *Understanding urban poverty: what the Poverty Reduction Strategy Papers tell us* which, like this paper, is available as a published working paper from www.earthprint.org or can be downloaded at no charge from www.iied.org/urban/

This paper takes me into areas where I have no professional training, and I hope that this does not mean that there are errors or that the positions of authors quoted or referenced are mis-represented. For people whose research is based more on qualitative techniques, it is often difficult to understand the reasons for what can be judged to be the inadequacies in the questions asked in large-scale quantitative surveys, and for what appear to be questionable assumptions made when interpreting their results to define and measure poverty. Much of the general literature on poverty lines is also not very accessible for non-economists, but this paper suggests that poverty definitions (including poverty lines) need to be scrutinized and questioned by a broader range of people, including urban poor organizations and the professionals who work with them.

I am especially grateful to Åsa Jonsson for her help and comments, and to friends and colleagues on the Urban Population Dynamics Panel at the US National Academy of Sciences that produced the book *Cities Transformed* noted above. I am also very grateful to a range of people for their comments on earlier drafts, including my colleagues Gordon McGranahan and Diana Mitlin, staff from the Indian NGO SPARC (Sheela Patel, Aditi Thorat, Devika Mahadevan), Gayatri Menon, Mark Montgomery (Population Council), James Garrett (IFPRI), Carole Rakodi (University of Birmingham) and Jane Bicknell (whose careful editing also improved the paper). All gave me valuable and detailed comments, which helped remove errors – but all remaining errors in this paper are solely my fault. I have also learnt much from working with SPARC and with James Garrett and Mark Montgomery.

Summary

There are good grounds for suggesting that the scale of urban poverty is systematically under-estimated in the official statistics produced and used by governments and international agencies.

Poverty lines are the main means by which poverty is defined and measured. The income level at which these are set is often too low in relation to housing costs in urban areas. Poverty lines often make no allowance for transport costs. They may allow too little for the cost of water for those who are not connected to piped systems and have to pay high prices to water vendors or kiosks. They often have unrealistic assumptions regarding the cost of meeting children's needs in urban areas.

The main reason for this is the inappropriate concepts used in setting poverty lines, especially in determining the income that individuals or households need for non-food essentials. This allowance for non-food essentials is usually based on what very poor households spend on non-food needs, not on what they require. Poverty lines are often not adjusted to accurately reflect variations in the costs of non-food essentials within nations – so the scale and depth of poverty is understated in places where these costs are particularly high (mainly cities). In the absence of adequate data, questionable assumptions and 'rules of thumb' are often used to set poverty lines that usually under-estimate the scale of urban poverty.

Other reasons for the under-estimation of urban poverty include:
- The over-reliance on poverty lines, which means a lack of attention to aspects of deprivation other than inadequate income, including inadequate, overcrowded and insecure housing, inadequate provision for water, sanitation, health care, emergency services and schools, vulnerability to stresses and shocks, and lack of the rule of law and respect for civil and political rights. This helps explain why the proportion of urban dwellers living in poverty is often much higher than that suggested by poverty statistics.
- The lack of knowledge of local contexts by those who define and measure poverty, in part reinforced by the lack of local data on living conditions and basic service provision. This often leads to urban poverty statistics that bear no relation to conditions on the ground.
- The definition of poverty and its measurement still being seen as something best left to experts. In most nations or cities, there is also no strong national or local debate about how poverty should be defined and measured. Even where there is, civil society (including those who are defined as 'poor') and local governments have little role in this. Yet those who are suffering deprivations caused by poverty within any country should feel that their needs and priorities are represented within official definitions and measurements (and the policies and actions that these should help create).

It might be assumed that poverty lines establish how many people have inadequate incomes to afford basic needs. But most poverty lines do not do so because they are not based on any study or data of the income level that individuals or households require to afford non-food essentials (including safe, secure housing, basic services including water and sanitation, health care, keeping children at school...).

Poverty lines (supposedly defining the income above or below which people can or cannot meet their needs) are usually based on two components:
- An allocation for food that is usually based on the cost of a minimum food basket or on the lowest income level at which households get sufficient calories.
- An allocation for non-food needs,[1] which is usually based on what a defined set of low-income households spend on non-food needs.

But what poor households spend on non-food needs is not a measure of whether their non-food needs are met. What low-income households of five or more persons spend on renting a single room (in which they

---

[1] Some poverty lines make no allowance for non-food needs, which is obviously invalid in any location where many or all non-food needs have to be paid for, i.e. virtually all urban centres.

all live), which lacks secure tenure and provision for piped water and sanitation is no indication of the amount actually required to meet their housing needs. Some poverty lines' allowance for non-food needs is very low, since it is based on what is spent on non-food needs by households whose *total* spending is the amount needed for food. In other words, households who will not eat enough if they spend anything on non-food needs. In other poverty lines, it is assumed that households who spend enough to get sufficient calories must have their non-food needs met. No research is done or data collected to see if their non-food needs are met. Also, no research is done to ascertain the income required for non-food needs.

Most poverty lines are set drawing on data from household expenditure surveys. If they are set based on national averages, this can lead to poverty lines that are too low for locations where most non-food needs are particularly expensive. In addition, without information on the income required to meet non-food needs in different locations, inadequate attention is given to adjustments for spatial variations. In larger and more prosperous cities, the costs of non-food needs such as housing, transport and basic services can be very high. This is especially so in cities that are poorly governed.

It is also not clear that the household surveys are representative of urban populations. In most low- and middle-income nations, much of the urban population are homeless (and sleep on the street or in public spaces) or live in illegal settlements and cheap boarding houses into which data gatherers are reluctant to go. For most illegal settlements, there are no maps, no official addresses and no household records.

Poverty lines can be set so low that households who live in tiny shacks built on pavements are apparently not 'poor'. This paper includes many examples of statistics suggesting that only 1-15 percent of a nation's urban population or a city's population is poor, when data on housing conditions and deficiencies in infrastructure and service provision show one-third to one-half living in poverty. In many nations said to have little urban poverty, urban infant and child mortality rates are 10-20 times what would be expected in places with little poverty.

The lack of attention to living conditions in poverty measurements (and, in poverty lines, to the income needed to afford adequate housing) is linked to the uncritical transfer of methods from high-income to low-income nations. Poverty lines were first used widely by governments in high-income nations when virtually everyone had access to health care and schools, and to accommodation that had provision for water, sanitation and electricity, independent of their income.[2] In most high-income nations, poverty lines were also one among several measures of deprivation. In low- and middle-income nations, poverty lines came to be applied as the principal or only method of measuring poverty – and this in situations where large sections of the (urban and rural) population lack access to schools and health care and to secure housing with access to water, sanitation and electricity. The methods for setting poverty lines that were first used in high-income nations are often reproduced by governments or international agencies in low- and middle-income nations without questioning their limitations, and mostly with less generosity - for instance, in the allowance made for non-food needs.

Some key questions that need to be asked regarding the setting of poverty lines:

In setting the income allowed for food, is this based on the kinds of food that low-income groups eat or on what experts think they need?	If the poverty line's allowance for food is based on the 'cheapest minimum food basket' defined by experts, this may be significantly less than the cost of what poor urban groups eat (influenced, for instance, by time shortages arising from long working hours and high fuel costs) or it may make unrealistically small allowances for higher quality food (for instance, meat or fish).

---

[2] There were exceptions, and in many instances, significant proportions of the low-income population did live in poor quality accommodation. But the extent of the deprivations linked to living conditions and lack of basic services, and the proportion of people affected were much lower than in low- and most middle-income nations today.

Is allowance made for non-food costs?	Many poverty lines are based only on the cost of food, especially 'extreme' poverty lines, even though in most urban contexts, many other needs have to be paid for.
If allowance is made for non-food costs, is this based on the real cost of non-food needs?	The allowance for non-food needs is generally based on what 'the poor' spend on non-food items regardless of whether or not their needs are met. Sometimes, this allowance is based only on the expenditure on non-food items of households whose total spending is just enough to get sufficient food (which is obviously not a measure of whether their non-food needs are met).
Is allowance made for the cost of housing?	Often not – or if allowance is made, usually imputed, because of the lack of relevant data from official surveys. Most poverty lines make very inadequate allowance for the income needed by households to avoid living in poverty in cities.
Is allowance made for spatial variations in the cost of non-food needs (especially for locations where non-food needs such as housing, transport and water are expensive)?	Often not. Where this is done, it is not based on data on the 'income needed to avoid poverty' in different locations. It may be based only on differences in food costs when spatial variations in the cost of non-food needs may be much larger. [3]
What allowance is made for children, when converting household data to individual data?	Children are often assumed to need only one-quarter or one-third of the income that adults need because their calorific requirements are less. But having one-third the calorific requirements of adults does not mean their food is one-third of the cost of adults' or that their non-food costs are one-third of an adult's costs. In many urban contexts, it is expensive for low-income households to keep their children at school and to get health care and afford medicines when they are sick. Children are more vulnerable to the health burdens associated with poverty and their health expenditures are likely to be higher, unless their illnesses and injuries go untreated.

Some of the limitations noted above are being addressed. In some nations, data on housing conditions and basic services are now seen as essential parts of defining and measuring poverty; in most nations, improved housing and living conditions are seen as important components of poverty reduction. In the last five years, allowances made in poverty lines for spatial variations in prices or costs within nations have become more common, and allowances for non-food needs have become less ungenerous. In many nations, there have been attempts to engage with 'the poor' and with civil society in discussing the nature of poverty, although with large differences in the extent to which these discussions have any influence on the way in which poverty is defined and measured. However, no study was found on what is perhaps the core issue for poverty lines in urban areas: the income levels that individuals and households need to avoid poverty, with particular attention to making sufficient allowance for non-food needs in the more expensive locations.

Even if poverty lines are set at levels that accurately reflect the income that poor urban dwellers need for food and non-food items, and adjusted to reflect spatial differences, they would still give an incomplete picture of deprivation. There is a need to widen poverty definitions to include aspects other than income or consumption – such as asset bases (and other means to reduce low-income people's vulnerability to stresses and shocks), housing conditions and tenure, access to services, the rule of law and respect for civil and political rights. These have importance not only for highlighting needs ignored by poverty lines

---

[3] Ironically, allowances for international agency staff to cover their daily costs (food and non-food) when working in low- and middle-income nations are adjusted by location within nations, with much more generous daily allowances for larger cities compared to smaller urban centres or rural areas – see Section III.

but also for helping to identify many more possibilities for poverty reduction and much expanded roles in poverty reduction for local governments, community organizations and local NGOs.

*This widening of poverty definitions is part of a more fundamental shift that is needed in development thinking. This shift is from official perceptions of 'poor people' as 'objects' of government policy to 'poor people' as citizens with rights and legitimate demands **who have** resources and capabilities that can contribute much to more effective poverty reduction.*

This shift implies:
- a greater engagement by those who define and measure poverty with the groups suffering deprivation;
- a greater focus on definitions and data that supports local action by governments and civil society. Most national governments and international agencies have supported decentralization and stronger local democracy but they have not supported the changes that these require in official statistical services to serve local plans and actions.

Household surveys that are based on representative samples for national populations are of little use to local poverty reduction programmes because they do not identify where those who are suffering from deprivation actually live. National statistical organizations should be serving the needs of local governments and civil society as well as national governments and international agencies. This includes ensuring that census data are available to local authorities and other local bodies in forms that allow their use in identifying and acting on deprivations (i.e. the availability of small-area data). It includes supporting local initiatives to generate the data needed for local action, including those that urban poor organizations can undertake themselves. There are now examples from many different nations and cities of city-wide 'slum' surveys, of very detailed 'slum' enumerations and of 'slum' mapping undertaken by urban poor organizations and local NGOs that provide strong information bases for housing improvement, regularizing tenure (and so making the inhabitants' housing more secure), and improving infrastructure and services. Many of these initiatives have also been catalysts for large-scale initiatives for poverty reduction, where representative organizations of the urban poor, local authorities and international agencies worked in partnership.

As in many aspects of development policy, there needs to be a shift among specialists from recommending 'what should be done' to recommending what local processes should be supported to influence what is done. One of the critical determinants of the success of poverty reduction initiatives is *the quality of the relationship between 'the poor' and the organizations or agencies* that have resources or powers that can help address one or more of the deprivations they suffer. Everyone who is concerned with the definition and measurement of poverty needs to consider how their work can support this.

This paper's focus on urban poverty does not mean that it is suggesting that urban poverty is worse than rural poverty, or that resources devoted to rural poverty reduction should be switched to urban areas. The scale and depth of rural poverty may also be under-estimated, with some of the factors that cause under-estimates for urban poverty also causing under-estimates for rural poverty. Many of the underlying causes of poverty affect both poor rural and urban populations. But this paper is suggesting that urban poverty reduction needs more attention; also, that new approaches are needed in defining and measuring poverty to support local action in which the organizations of the urban poor have a central role.

I. INTRODUCTION

This paper's principal interest is in whether the poverty statistics used by governments and international agencies accurately reflect the scale and nature of deprivation in urban areas. This includes an interest in identifying hidden influences and assumptions within poverty definitions that affect who is identified as being poor. Its primary focus is on reviewing how poverty lines are defined, since these are the main means by which poverty is defined and measured in most low- and middle-income nations. In this, its interest is in whether these poverty lines are appropriate for identifying and measuring poverty in urban populations; it is not seeking to compare the scale and depth of urban poverty relative to rural poverty. It suggests that in many nations, the scale of urban poverty is under-estimated because of inappropriate definitions and assumptions, often reinforced by inadequate data.

a. How different definitions influence the scale of poverty

Defining and measuring poverty should be central to any government's policies, since this helps identify who is in need and helps establish what actions are required to address their needs. It should be at the centre of the policies and interests of any aid agency or development bank (whose very existence is largely justified by their contribution to reducing poverty). Obviously, it is important to get the definition and measurement right; also, for those suffering deprivations caused by poverty within any country to feel that their needs and priorities are represented within this definition and measurement (and the policies and actions that these help create).

Defining poverty might also be considered as relatively simple: there is not much disagreement that everyone needs sufficient food, access to services such as health care and schools and a secure home with adequate provision for water and sanitation. It is accepted that 'adequate' income is the primary means by which individuals or households can meet these needs – especially in urban areas, where there is generally less scope for self-production. So a poverty line set at a particular income level can be used to measure who is poor (although with allowance made for self-production). This means that those who have sufficient income for a set of goods and services considered as 'needs' are non-poor and those who do not are poor. There are needs other than sufficient income such as the rule of law and respect for civil and political rights (and the means to ensure both are realized) – although these are usually not seen as part of poverty (even if inadequate rule of law and contravention of civil and political rights are often associated with poverty and may be major causes or contributors to poverty). There is also a recognition that asset bases are important for allowing low-income individuals or households to avoid or better cope with poverty, although very few poverty definitions include any provision for assets.

But there is no agreement on how best to define and measure poverty. During the late 1990s, there were at least four figures for the proportion of Kenya's urban population who were poor, ranging from 1 to 49 percent.[4] In the Philippines, in 2000, the proportion of the national population with below poverty line incomes was 12 percent, 25 percent, 40 percent or 45–46 percent, depending on which poverty line is chosen.[5] In Ethiopia, the proportion of the urban population with below poverty line incomes in 1995/96 could have been 49 percent, 33 percent or 18 percent, depending on what figure was used for the average calorific requirement per person.[6]

These very large differences in the proportion of the national or urban population considered poor are the result of different definitions of poverty. These differences usually lie in how to define the income that individuals or households need to avoid being poor, especially with regard to non-food essentials. However, the example from Ethiopia shows how influential the choice of which figure to use for food requirements can be. These differences can also be caused by whether the definition and measurement of poverty includes some consideration of basic service provision or housing quality, and the quality or appropriateness of the data from which these draw.

---

[4] Sahn and Stifel 2003 suggest 1.2 percent in 1998; official statistics suggested three different figures in 1997: hardcore poverty 7.6 percent; food poverty 38.3 percent; absolute poverty 49 percent.
[5] See World Bank 2002a.
[6] World Bank 1999a.

If the different methods available for defining and measuring poverty produced similar figures for the scale and depth of poverty, then this concern for definitional issues would be less relevant. For instance, Kanbur and Squire 2001 suggest that: "Although different methods of defining and measuring poverty inevitably identify different groups as poor, the evidence suggests that the differences may not be that great" (page 216). But this is not so if one definition of poverty suggests that 1 percent of Kenya's urban population are poor and another suggests that 49 percent are poor. *Clearly, the choice of what definition to use matters if one definition means a very small minority of the urban population (or national population) are poor while another means that half the urban population (or national population) are poor.*

The choice of which definition to use to measure poverty inevitably influences responses by governments and international agencies: if 1.2 percent of Kenya's urban population or 2.3 percent of Zimbabwe's urban population or 0.9 percent of Senegal's urban population were poor in the mid- or late 1990s, as suggested by Sahn and Stifel 2003, clearly, addressing urban poverty is not a priority as each of these nations has a high proportion of their rural population suffering from poverty, and most of their population is in rural areas. But, if between one-third and one-half of these nations' urban populations are facing serious deprivations (which is actually the case, as discussed later), and most of the growth in poverty is taking place in urban areas (which may be the case),[7] the needs of the urban poor deserve far more attention.

With many governments and most international agencies now making more explicit commitments to reducing poverty through Poverty Reduction Strategies and through focusing on the Millennium Development Goals, the question of how urban poverty is defined and measured has great relevance to whether these will see urban poverty as worth addressing. A companion paper to this one, by Diana Mitlin, reviews the attention given to urban poverty in recent Poverty Reduction Strategy Papers, and this suggests considerable ambiguity with regard to whether urban poverty should get much attention.[8] The authors whose unrealistically low estimates for urban poverty rates were noted earlier (Sahn and Stifel 2003) certainly want more attention to rural poverty, and worry that too much attention will be given to urban areas; in their discussion of how to meet the Millennium Development Goals in Africa, they do not even mention the Goal of significantly improving the lives of slum dwellers, as if this was irrelevant to Africa.

Much of the general literature on poverty does not recognize that there are particular 'urban' characteristics that most urban areas share, which influence the scale and depth of poverty there (see, for instance, World Bank 2000). Much of the general literature on poverty also does not draw on the literature on urban problems. This means that key characteristics of urban areas (or of some urban areas or of some districts within urban areas[9]) are not taken into account in the definitions of poverty or in its

---

[7] UN statistics on urban change suggest that virtually all the increases in population in low- and middle-income nations will be in urban areas over the next 25–30 years (United Nations 2002). I would be more cautious, in that the extent to which a nation urbanizes is strongly influenced by its economic performance (see UNCHS 1996, Satterthwaite 2002a), and many low-income, predominantly rural nations may have too poor an economic performance between 2000 and 2025 to mean that most of the population growth will be in urban areas. There are some sources suggesting that sub-Saharan Africa continued to urbanize without economic growth during the 1980s and 1990s (see Fay and Opal 2000, World Bank 1999b), but since their analysis was not based on recent census data (they were based on reviews of urban population statistics that were mostly projections and estimates because of the lack of census data), their validity can be questioned. Much of the growth in levels of urbanization that they detected in sub-Saharan Africa was the result of an assumption that urbanization levels would go on rising within the methodology used for making estimates and projections, when there were no census data.

[8] Mitlin 2004.

[9] There are obvious economic, demographic and usually social and political characteristics that distinguish urban areas from rural areas, and that have importance for defining and measuring poverty – for instance, as discussed in this paper, higher monetary costs for many essential goods and services, more monetized housing and land for housing markets, and fewer possibilities for accessing or using resources at no monetary cost. However, the great variations between urban areas should be recognized – for instance, many small urban centres may have many rural characteristics (and have more in common with most large villages than with major cities). Similarly, some rural areas have urban characteristics; in some nations, highly urbanized settlements in terms of employment structure, house type and density may still be classified as rural – see Satterthwaite and Tacoli 2002 and 2003).

measurement. Combine a lack of knowledge (or data) about housing and living conditions with little or no allowance for the cost of non-food necessities in urban areas (or particular cities), and it is possible to produce statistics that so under-state the scale and depth of urban poverty as to render them invalid, whatever definition is being used. This is reinforced by the lack of knowledge by poverty specialists of urban contexts; anyone with any knowledge of urban centres in Kenya, Senegal or Zimbabwe would know that the urban poverty statistics noted above were wrong. This paper has other examples of urban poverty statistics that are at odds with well-documented local realities, and other examples where the statistics appear faulty.

One other reason behind this capacity to produce questionable statistics is the lack of engagement by those producing and using official (government and international agency) poverty statistics with 'the poor' who are meant to be the object of their concern. Given the likely influence of poverty definitions on the policies and resource allocations of most governments and international agencies, one would expect the definition of poverty and its measurement to be one of the key topics for public discussion and debate within each country (and since this paper's interest is in urban poverty, in each city or town). Such public debate is also important to guard against inappropriate definitions of 'need'. But there is little evidence of such a public debate in most low-income nations.[10] This may be in part because, in many nations, there is little link between the measurement of poverty and the capacity or willingness of government agencies to reduce it. Low-income groups will have little interest in being 'defined as poor' if this implies no action to help them. However, part of the reason is the difficulty for non-specialists to engage in this discussion – and to identify all the influences on the definition and measurement of poverty.

b. Rural versus urban

As in the other published work of IIED's Human Settlements Programme on urban poverty, this paper is not recommending that funds allocated to rural poverty reduction be redirected to urban poverty reduction; it may be that the scale and depth of rural poverty is also under-estimated and mis-represented by conventional poverty statistics. The failure of consumption-based poverty lines to capture the extent and nature of deprivation in rural areas may actually be greater than in urban areas, because so much rural deprivation is related to lack of assets (especially fertile land) and lack of access to services, not lack of income. Neither is this paper seeking to make judgements about the relative scale or depth of 'urban' poverty compared to 'rural' poverty. Where comparisons are made between the two, or in the ways in which they are understood, it is to highlight how the understanding or measurement of poverty in urban areas (or of poverty in general) has failed to take due note of costs or of forms of deprivation that are evident in some (or most) urban areas. The paper's suggestion that too little attention has been given to addressing the health burden associated with 'poverty' probably has as much, if not more, relevance for rural populations as for urban populations.

However, this paper does take issue with much of the general literature on 'poverty' or the writings of rural specialists who discuss 'urban poverty', yet fail to understand how urban contexts generate or exacerbate poverty. Much of the general literature on poverty assumes that there is an 'urban bias' in international agencies' priorities that remains unproven – and is certainly at odds with our analyses, which show a very low priority given by most international agencies to urban poverty reduction.[11] There is also the need for understandings of poverty that recognize the multiple linkages between rural and urban areas; IIED's Human Settlements Programme has long sought to promote a greater understanding of rural–urban linkages, including those relevant to understanding poverty.[12] In addition, as Wratten 1995 notes, discussions about whether rural or urban poverty is worse can distract attention from the structural determinants that affect both. These include those internal to the nation, such as the distribution of assets, socially constructed constraints to opportunity based on class, gender, race and age, and macro-economic policies (although these are often influenced by external agencies). They include those that are external

---

[10] There are important exceptions – for instance, the lively debate in India about the setting of poverty lines.
[11] See Satterthwaite 1997b and 2001, Hardoy, Mitlin and Satterthwaite 2001.
[12] See, for instance, Tacoli 1998 and many of the papers in Vol 10 No 1 (1998) and Vol 15 No 1 (2003) of *Environment and Urbanization*.

to low- and middle-income nations, such as terms of trade, external debt burdens, and the barriers around the world's wealthiest consumer markets and unfair practices within these markets. Discussions regarding how much farmers in low-income nations lose out to trade barriers and subsidies to rich-world farmers usually forget how much this also affects the urban-based enterprises that serve export agriculture (transport, credit, farm inputs, storage, processing...) or that rely on rural households' demand for goods and services.

What this paper does recommend is a greater attention to understanding and measuring urban poverty in ways that better capture the scale and nature of deprivation in each location, and better serve poverty reduction, including supporting the role of local (governmental and civil society) actors. The case for more attention to urban poverty reduction is also reinforced by the evidence that much can be done to reduce urban poverty, drawing only on the resources and powers available to urban governments and increasing the scope permitted to the actions of low-income groups and their organizations and federations.[13] Surprisingly, much of the literature on poverty hardly mentions these.

II. UNDER-STATING URBAN POVERTY

a. The gaps between poverty statistics and data on living conditions and health status

If the term poverty is taken to mean human needs that are not met, then most of the estimates for the scale of urban poverty in low- and middle-income countries appear too low.[14] Statistics produced by international agencies consistently suggest that three-quarters or more of the urban population in low- and middle-income countries do not live in poverty. For instance, a publication by the Overseas Development Council in the USA in 1989 decided that only 130 million of the 'poorest poor' within low- and middle-income nations lived in urban areas (Leonard 1989), which meant that more than nine out of ten of their urban population were not among the poorest poor. World Bank estimates for 1988 suggested that there were 330 million 'poor' people living in urban areas in low- and middle-income countries (World Bank 1991), which meant that more than three-quarters of their urban population were not 'poor' on that date.[15] The 1999/2000 World Development Report (World Bank 1999b) suggested that there were 495 million 'urban poor' by the year 2000, which meant that three-quarters of the urban population were 'not poor'. But many national and city studies show that 40 to 65 percent of a nation's urban population or a major city's population have incomes too low to allow them to meet their needs,[16] although there are too few such studies to allow estimates of the scale of urban poverty for all low- and middle-income nations. The World Bank estimates for the scale of urban poverty for 1988 and 2000 suggest that there was no increase in the proportion of the urban population living in poverty between these years. Yet, many studies show increasing proportions of nations' urban populations suffering from poverty during the 1980s or 1990s, relating to poor economic performance and/or structural adjustment,[17] although, again, there are too few to be able to generalize for all low- and middle-income nations.

In general, the proportion of urban dwellers living in poverty (i.e. in poor quality, overcrowded and often insecure housing lacking adequate provision for water, sanitation, drainage.....) and exposed to very high levels of environmental health risk is higher than the proportion defined as poor by poverty lines in sub-Saharan Africa and some other low- and middle-income nations.[18] For instance, considerably more than one-quarter of the urban population in most low- and middle-income nations live in poor quality (and

---

[13] See the October 2001 issue of *Environment and Urbanization* and Satterthwaite 2002b; also, the case studies in Mitlin and Satterthwaite 2004.

[14] This first section is an updated version of the first section in Satterthwaite 1997a.

[15] Assuming around 1.35 billion urban dwellers in low- and middle-income nations on that date; see UNCHS 1996.

[16] See Annex 2; also Tabatabai with Fouad 1993 for a review of national studies from many countries, Bijlmakers, Bassett and Sanders 1998 for Zimbabwe, Islam, Huda, Narayan and Rana 1997 for Bangladesh, Ghosh, Ahmad and Maitra 1994 for four cities in India, Aegisson 2001 for Angola.

[17] See, for instance, Kanji 1995, Latapí and González de la Rocha 1995, Minujin 1995, Moser, Herbert and Makonnen 1993, and Maxwell, Levin, Armar-Klemesdu et al 1998.

[18] The official UN statistics (WHO/UNICEF 2000) may appear not to show this, but this is because they are not based on data showing who has adequate provision, as this source discusses and as shown by UN Habitat 2003a.

often insecure or illegal) homes with inadequate provision for water, sanitation and drainage.[19] If the estimate for the number of 'poor' urban dwellers was based on the number living in poor quality housing with a lack of basic infrastructure and services, then at least 600 million were poor in 1990, with the numbers likely to have increased significantly during the 1990s.[20] For instance, a detailed review of provision for water and sanitation in urban areas suggested that there were at least 650 million urban dwellers lacking adequate provision for water and at least 850 million lacking adequate provision for sanitation in Africa, Asia and Latin America (UN Habitat 2003a).[21]

It is not only international statistics that seem to under-estimate the proportion of poor urban households but also many national statistics. For instance, the suggestion that 2.1 percent of Zimbabwe's urban population was poor in 1994 (Sahn and Stifel 2003) bears no relation to the documentation showing the scale of urban poverty in the early 1990s and the large increase in its scale and depth from large price rises, retrenchments and declines in the amount spent by poorer groups on food (see Kanji 1995) – or the official survey in 1996 showing 46 percent of urban households being poor, including 25 percent who could not meet their basic nutritional requirements (Zimbabwe, Government of, quoted in Bijlmakers, Bassett and Sanders 1998). There is also a considerable literature on the very poor living conditions that much of Zimbabwe's urban population endure.[22]

The suggestion that 1.5 percent of Kenya's urban population was poor in 1988 and that 1.2 percent was poor in 1998 (Sahn and Stifel 2003) also bears no relation to figures drawn from other sources – for instance, the official survey in 1997 which found that 49 percent of the urban population was poor (Kenya, Government of, 2002) – or to the very poor conditions under which a large proportion of the population of the two largest cities live,[23] or to the very high under-five mortality rates within the informal settlements in which half of Nairobi's population lives (APHRC 2002). For Senegal, the suggestion that less than 1 percent of its urban population was poor in 1997 (Sahn and Stifel 2003) hardly fits with the very poor conditions in which a significant proportion of the urban population lives, or with the official figure from 2001 which suggested that 44–59 percent of the urban population was poor, depending on the zone (Senegal, Government of 2002). Many other figures presented by Sahn and Stifel 2003 can be questioned – for instance, that only 5.4 percent of Burkina Faso's urban population was poor in 1999 or that only 6.8 percent of Ghana's urban population was poor in 1998.

Drawing from other sources, it is difficult to take seriously the suggestion that less than 2 percent of China's urban population was below the poverty line in 1994 (World Bank 1999b)[24] or that 14.3 percent of Bangladesh's urban population was below the poverty line in 1995/96 (World Bank 2000). Or that only 3.8 percent of Accra's population was poor in 1998/99 (as claimed by Ghana, Government of, 2000),[25] or that only 9 percent of Vietnam's urban population was poor in 1998 (Vietnam, Socialist

---

[19] Cairncross, Hardoy and Satterthwaite 1990, WHO 1992 and 1999, Hardoy, Mitlin and Satterthwaite 2001 and UN–Habitat 2003a.

[20] Cairncross, Hardoy and Satterthwaite 1990, WHO 1992, 1999, UN Habitat 2003b.

[21] Official United Nations statistics on provision for water and sanitation are often cited to show that provision is much better in urban areas than in rural areas, but these statistics do not show who has adequate provision; see Hardoy, Mitlin and Satterthwaite 2001 and UN Habitat 2003a.

[22] For instance, Chitekwe and Mitlin 2001, Potts and Mutambirwa 1991, Schlyter 1990 and Rakodi and Withers 1995.

[23] For Nairobi, see Lamba 1994, Alder 1995, APHRC 2002 and Weru 2004; for Mombasa, see Rakodi, Gatabaki-Kamau and Devas 2000.

[24] See GHK and IIED 2004 for a discussion of how urban poverty is under-estimated in China - in part because of unrealistically low poverty lines, in part because 100 million 'temporary' migrants who live and work in urban areas are classified as 'rural'. This study also noted that increasing the poverty line used in a recent study by 25 percent would more than double the proportion of the urban population below the poverty line (from 4.7 to 11.1 percent); increasing the poverty line by 50 percent would mean that 20.1 percent of China's urban population would be below the poverty line.

[25] See, for instance, Devas and Korboe 2000; a government living standards survey had suggested that 23 percent of Accra's population was poor, although this is likely to be based on a different poverty line from that used in 2000, and there is no evidence of conditions having improved during the 1990s to so radically reduce poverty levels. See also Songsore and McGranahan 1993 and Maxwell, Levin, Armar-Klemesu et al 1998.

Republic of, 2002).[26] Official figures for the proportion of Phnom Penh's population with below poverty line incomes in 1999 (9.7 percent or 14.6 percent depending on which survey is used – see Cambodia, Kingdom of, 2002) bear little relation to the proportion living in illegal or informal settlements or crowded tenements with very inadequate provision for water and sanitation, which is estimated at around 40 percent of the city's population (Asian Coalition for Housing Rights 2001).

Annex 1 includes details of how poverty is defined and measured in 35 nations, while Annex 2 gives statistics for the proportion of the urban population with below poverty line incomes in 41 nations (also including, where available, statistics for individual cities). Many of the figures on levels of urban poverty for nations or for particular cities in these Annexes are much lower than the proportion of people living in very poor quality housing that lacks basic infrastructure or services. Some nations also have surprisingly low proportions of their urban population apparently suffering from poverty, yet have very high infant and child mortality rates in urban areas (see Annex with figures for 53 nations).

- In Tanzania, in 2000, less than one-quarter of the urban population was poor according to official statistics, yet infant mortality rates in urban areas in 1996 were 82 per 1,000 live births, and for child mortality, 42 per 1,000 live births.
- In Dar es Salaam, Tanzania's largest city, according to official statistics, 17.6 percent of the population was poor in 2000/2001, but the under-five mortality rate in the city in 1999 was 173 per 1,000 live births (at least ten times what could be expected for a city with more than four-fifths of its population not poor); the prevalence of diarrhoea was also very high (Tanzania, Government of, 2002a).[27]
- In Burkina Faso, 16.5 percent of the urban population was poor in 1998 according to official statistics, yet infant mortality rates were 66 per 1,000 live births and child mortality rates 67 per 1,000 live births in urban areas in that same year.[28]

Cameroon and Togo are among the other nations in Annex 3 whose relatively high infant and child mortality rates in urban areas seem at odds with the relatively low proportions of their urban populations defined as poor. The figures given above and those in Annex 3 are averages for entire urban populations or for all city inhabitants. Infant and child mortality rates will be much higher for low-income groups; in Kenya, infant and child mortality rates in the low-income settlements in Nairobi, where around half the city's population lives, were nearly twice those of the Kenya-wide urban average (APHRC 2002).

It may also be that the scale of under-nutrition in urban areas is not fully recognized in many nations. The persons said to be 'poor' by poverty lines are those whose incomes fall below what the official agency thinks is the amount they need to feed themselves, but there are many ways in which this can be under-estimated. It is clear that, in general, there is less under-nutrition in urban areas than in rural areas. An analysis of DHS data found that children's height-for-age was greater in urban areas than in rural areas in all but one case (Uzbekistan), but that the 'urban advantage' of weight-for-age was smaller and, for six nations, weight-for-age was higher in rural areas than in urban areas.[29] According to a review of available data by the International Food Policy Research Institute (IFPRI), childhood mortality, stunting and under-weight are generally lower in urban than in rural areas, whereas acute malnutrition or wasting (as measured by low weight-for-height) and morbidity from infectious diseases are often higher in urban areas. However, there is considerable heterogeneity in poverty, morbidity, mortality and nutritional status in urban areas and, generally, the intra-urban differences are greater than the rural–urban differences.[30] Thus, the problem of under-nutrition among lower-income groups in urban areas may be more serious

---

[26] See, for instance, Wust, Bolay and Thi Ngoc Du 2002 on conditions in Ho Chi Minh City.

[27] The document that claimed that only 17.6 percent of Dar es Salaam was poor also noted that 30 percent of households lived in one room, that 60,000 lived in valleys that exposed them to the risk of floods and diseases, and that 15,000–20,000 lived on the streets (Tanzania, Government of, 2002a). Recent documentation of provision for water and sanitation in Dar es Salaam shows that far more than 17.6 percent face very serious deficiencies (Glockner, Mkanga and Ndezi 2004).

[28] Data on mortality rates from Population Reports, Johns Hopkins Bloomberg School of Public Health 2002. Basic data from the DHS.

[29] Montgomery, Stren, Cohen and Reed 2003.

[30] Ruel, Garrett, Morris et al 1998.

than is assumed, but hidden in any urban average because of the concentration of well-fed middle- and upper-income groups in urban areas.

The 'urban advantage' for nutrition may also not be so great in many nations; for instance, the differences between rural and urban areas in the prevalence of severe malnutrition in children in Bangladesh in 2000 were not as large as might have been expected, if there is urban bias (UNICEF 2000).[31]

The deficiencies in provision for water and sanitation in urban areas are also often under-stated. Most documents on provision for water and sanitation greatly under-estimate the extent and depth of the inadequacies in provision in urban areas because of inappropriate assumptions and poor data. For instance, data on the proportion of the urban population that 'has access to piped water supplies' or a latrine is often taken to mean the proportion with 'adequate provision' – but this is not so if each water tap or latrine is shared by dozens or hundreds of people (as is often the case in urban areas), and the water in the pipe is of poor quality and with only intermittent supplies (as is also often the case).[32] It is also common for inappropriate judgements to be made about the quality of housing based on the limited data available – for instance, the weight given to data on flooring materials which, in many urban areas, is unlikely to be a valid indicator of living conditions – or, more importantly, of the level of health risk for occupants from biological pathogens, chemical pollutants and physical hazards (the main means by which poor housing quality translates into illness, injury and premature death – see Hardoy, Mitlin and Satterthwaite 2001).[33]

Thus, there are many nations where the proportion of urban dwellers who are poor according to official poverty definitions is significantly less than the proportion living in poverty, or significantly less than the proportion with health outcomes or nutritional levels that one would assume are associated with poverty. This also true for particular cities. This may be because poverty lines are set too low in relation to the costs of housing and essential services, as discussed in Sections III and IV. Or it may be related more to the incapacity of public, private or non-profit institutions as discussed in Section V.

III. THE UNREALISTIC CRITERIA USED TO SET POVERTY LINES

a. The increased attention to poverty

Poverty is getting more attention in the literature on development than it did 15 years ago. The discussion of poverty has also widened beyond consumption-based definitions, to include discussions of the lack of basic service provision and other deprivations, although this is not so much new as a return to what was recognized in the 1970s.[34] This greater attention to poverty is both in the literature that is published and in the 'grey' literature of reports produced by international agencies and national governments. Most international agencies and many governments are also more explicit about their commitment to reducing poverty, especially through the Poverty Reduction Strategy Papers that most low- and many middle-income nations have developed (see Mitlin 2004). An increasing number of governments and international agencies are also incorporating a commitment to meeting the Millennium Development

---

[31] For boys, 3.6 percent of the rural population and 3.4 percent of the urban population; for girls 5.9 percent of the rural population and 4.5 percent of the urban population. The prevalence of severe malnutrition in boys in 'slums' in Chittagong and Dhaka was more than twice the average for urban areas; for girls, it was only slightly higher (UNICEF 2000).

[32] See Hardoy, Mitlin and Satterthwaite 2001 and UN Habitat 2003a for more details.

[33] Obviously, this is a particularly inappropriate indicator for cities or for urban districts with multi-storey housing, since any floor above the ground floor cannot have a 'dirt floor', but levels of overcrowding and inadequacies in infrastructure and services and in the conditions of the building can be very serious in tenements and cheap boarding houses that are within multi-storey housing.

[34] In large part, this only returns to the 'basic needs' discussions of the 1970s, where great stress was put by many international agencies and some governments on the need to improve basic service provision (see, for instance, ILO 1976, Chenery, Ahluwalia, Bell et al 1974, Streeten 1981, Sandbrook 1982), although this was less explicitly linked to the discourse on poverty.

Goals in their plans and programmes, and this includes specific goals and targets related to poverty.[35] Most governments and international agencies also acknowledge that poverty has many dimensions – i.e. that it is more than hunger or insufficient income to purchase food – and also the need to improve 'basic service provision' as part of poverty reduction.

However, the way that poverty is defined and measured in most low-income and many middle-income nations remains rooted in questionable assumptions about what 'poverty' is, and is often locked in 19th century attitudes concerning the needs and rights of the 'poor'. In most nations, poverty is still defined and measured through consumption-based poverty lines, despite the recognition of how inadequately these capture many aspects of deprivation. As shown in Annex 1, many poverty lines are still based entirely or mostly on the cost of a 'minimum food basket', giving inadequate or no consideration to non-food needs, yet much urban poverty is related to the inability of individuals or households to afford non-food items.

It is also assumed that poverty data is needed for national decision-making, not for local decision-making. Data on poverty is still drawn primarily from expenditure surveys based on 'representative samples of national populations' (and these are often managed by external organizations). These are of little use to local governments and other local institutions who are meant to help reduce poverty, because they give no data on who within each locality is poor and what deprivations they suffer. At least within discussions of urban poverty, the important potential role of local governments in poverty reduction is recognized, but most national statistical services and the international agencies' support for these do little to support the collection of data that serves local governments' poverty reduction potential.

Questions also need to be raised about whether the samples used in these surveys really are representative for urban areas, especially for those sections of the urban poor who are most difficult to include in surveys. Do the household surveys from which data are drawn for setting poverty lines or assessing living conditions contain a representative sample from urban areas? It is always difficult to get a good sample frame of urban dwellers, and those who are left out are mostly going to be poor – those who are homeless (for instance, sleeping in public places or open spaces), those who are temporary (for instance, construction workers and their families who live on the construction sites – see Patel 1990), those who are 'visitors', those who sleep in workplaces and those who live in illegal settlements for which there are no official data or maps (which, in many cities, represents 20–50 percent of their population). In many instances, it is also difficult to get data from tenants (see Weru 2004) and to identify families or individuals living in back rooms of residences that look as though they only hold one household (and perhaps these other families or individuals are not 'allowed' to live there, so will seek to conceal their existence). It is almost certainly frightening for those undertaking the surveys to go into most illegal settlements or areas with tenements and cheap boarding houses (which often have a reputation for being dangerous places for outsiders to visit). Do sample frames really ensure that, if half a city's population live in illegal settlements for which there are no official maps or data, then half the sample is drawn from these settlements, with care to ensure that the diversity among these settlements is represented? If not, are measures taken to try to compensate for this and, if they are, are they sufficient? If the urban poor are considerably under-represented in household surveys, how much does this limit the validity of rural:urban comparisons?

Rarely is there any scope for dialogue with the population about their needs and priorities. Even if this is changing, the dialogue is not likely to influence how poverty is defined and measured – see Mitlin 2004.

---

[35] The Millennium Development Goals include: achieving universal primary education by 2015; greatly reducing infant and child mortality (reducing under-five mortality by two-thirds between 1990–2015; reducing maternal mortality by three-quarters between 1990 and 2015; halving the number of people without safe drinking water, adequate incomes and food intakes by 2015 compared to 1990; significantly improving the lives of at least 100 million 'slum' dwellers by 2020 (which includes increasing the proportion of people with 'improved' sanitation and secure tenure); halting and beginning to reverse the spread of Aids, malaria and other major diseases; and promoting gender equality. But the extent to which these help reduce urban poverty depends on the extent to which governments and international agencies acknowledge the urban components of the deficits in terms of malnutrition and inadequate income, and in provision for water, sanitation, maternal and child health care.

In defining and measuring poverty, concepts and methods developed and used in high-income nations are borrowed and applied with too little consideration of whether they are appropriate. It is not the same to measure poverty based only on consumption for nations where most of those with below poverty line incomes still had access to safe housing with basic infrastructure and services, and to schools, health care, protection from the law and political voice as for those nations where the majority of those with below poverty line incomes have few if any of these. In high-income nations, poverty lines were also introduced within lively political discussions and debates about their appropriateness; there is little evidence within most low- and middle-income nations of comparable debates, including space for the urban organizations and federations of the urban poor to question these. Poverty lines in most high-income nations were also developed to allow government provision of subsistence incomes or accommodation or other entitlements to those who had below poverty line incomes. In most low- and middle-income nations, there are few if any entitlements for those who have below poverty line incomes and even where entitlements exist, many of the poorest groups cannot access them.[36]

That poverty lines have limitations is widely accepted. For instance, Kanbur and Squire 2001 note that "…conventional measures of poverty draw heavily on the statistical information contained in household surveys, combined with a more or less arbitrary cut-off separating the poor from the non-poor" (page 204). That there are limitations in the ways in which provision is made for non-food needs is also recognized. As Ravallion 1998 notes: "Of all the data that goes into measuring poverty, setting the non-food component of the poverty line is probably the most contentious" (page 17). The rest of this section examines the extent to which poverty lines are set in ways that can under-state the incidence and depth of urban poverty.

b. The inadequate allowance made for non-food needs

Most poverty lines use criteria to set the income level below which individuals or households are defined as 'poor' that give little attention to non-food needs.[37] Yet, in urban areas, especially the larger and/or more prosperous urban centres, the income level required to satisfy non-food needs is likely to be particularly high. One of the defining characteristics of cities is that access to goods and services is highly monetized. This includes access to housing, whether this is rented or self-built (with the housing costs being the cost of the land, the building and the materials used, any payments needed to get connections to utility networks and, where credit is used, the cost of credit). It includes access to safe water (often expensive for low-income groups) and a place to defecate (large sections of the urban poor do not have toilets in their homes and, in many locations, their only access is through pay-toilets).[38] It includes transport costs (income-earners getting to and from work, children getting to and from school, all family members getting to and from services such as health care); these can be particularly expensive for the poorer groups who live in peripheral locations because this cheapens their housing costs or allows them more space and/or possibilities for becoming house owners. It includes the costs that have to be paid for health care and medicines and for schools – both of which can be costly for low-income groups, as described in Section IV. Of course, there are also other costs, such as fuels (and, where it is available, electricity) and clothing. There are often payments that have to be made to community organizations, and costs of meeting social obligations; tragically, the cost of funerals has become particularly onerous for a large proportion of low-income families because of so much premature death (of infants and children; also of adults, with death rates boosted by AIDS).

Poverty lines are generally derived from data on the cost of a 'minimum food basket' in terms of calorific intake, with some additional amount added for non-food needs. The review of how poverty is defined in Tabatabai with Fouad 1993 is particularly interesting, as it gives figures for the incidence of poverty for urban and rural populations for a great range of nations. For many, there are also details of how the poverty line was set. This shows that, until 1990, many poverty lines were set based only on the

---

[36] For instance, many entitlements are only accessed if the individual or household has a legal address yet large sections of the urban population are homeless or live in homes in illegal settlements which have no legal address.
[37] There are also debates and discussions regarding the adequacy of the methods used to establish or estimate the incomes needed to afford sufficient food – see Ravallion 1998, Wratten 1995 and Reddy and Pogge 2003, for instance.
[38] Hardoy, Mitlin and Satterthwaite 2001, UN Habitat 2003a.

cost of a 'minimum' food basket, considered to constitute an adequate diet in calorific terms. For those poverty lines that make allowances for non-food items, generally this was either based on an assumption that food expenditure would be 70–85 percent of total expenditure, or based on what a reference group of 'poor' households spent on non-food items (with this group varying – for instance, sometimes the lowest 10 percent or lowest quintile). Thus, if allowance was made for non-food needs, it was assumed that only a small proportion of a poor household's income was required for this. The surveys from which data were drawn did not consider whether this small upward adjustment actually allowed poor people to afford non-food needs. Many studies show low-income urban households spending much more than 30 percent of their income on non-food items and still living in poverty,[39] which suggests that the income required to pay for non-food needs was higher than that allowed for in setting poverty lines.

Over the last ten years, there is some evidence of more generous allowances made for non-food items. This can be seen in many of the poverty lines in the most recently available documentation for individual nations on poverty assessments or Poverty Reduction Strategy Papers which show a larger upward adjustment for 'absolute poverty lines' relative to food poverty lines (see Table 1). Some upward adjustments remain low – for instance, for Ghana for 1998/99, which may explain why there was apparently so little 'poverty' in Accra (yet, as noted earlier, housing and living conditions and basic service provision for large sections of Accra's population remain very poor). The fact that the proportion of urban dwellers living in poverty is much higher than the proportion defined as poor by official poverty lines was noted earlier for Burkina Faso, Tanzania and Vietnam; these are also nations with relatively small allowances for non-food needs in their poverty lines.

Table 1: Levels of urban poverty according to 'upper poverty lines', where some allowance is made for non-food needs and the extent of the upward adjustment of 'food poverty' lines to take account of non-food needs

Nation	Poverty line as a multiple of 'minimum food basket' costs	Proportion of the urban population below the poverty line
Burkina Faso (1998)	1.0	16.5
Sri Lanka (1995/96)	1.2	25.0
Madagascar (1999)	1.21	52.1
Ghana (1998/99)	1.29	19.4
Mauritania (1996)	1.32	26.8
Chad (1995/96)	1.3	35.0-39.3
Tanzania (2000/01)	1.37	17.6-25.8
Vietnam (1998)	1.39	9.0
Zambia (1998)	1.44	56.0
Niger (1994)	1.5	52.0
Malawi (1997/98)	1.5	54.9
Swaziland (1995)	1.51	45.2
Yemen (1998)	1.52	30.8
Cameroon (2001)	1.54	17.9
Gambia (1998)	1.66	15.0
China (1998/99)	1.66	4.7
Mozambique (1996/97)	1.66	62.0
Nepal (1995/6)	1.67	23.0
Honduras (1999)	1.68	57.3
Ivory Coast (1998)	1.7	

---

[39] See, for instance, Grootaert 1996 for Côte d'Ivoire, Ghosh, Ahmad and Maitra 1994 for four cities in India, Maxwell, Levin, Armar-Klemesu et al 1998 for Accra, Dinye 1995 for a sample of households within a low-income settlement in Kumasi, Malawi, Government of, 1994 for Lilongwe, Blantyre and Mzuzu cities, Huq 1996 for the urban poor in Bangladesh; see also Section IV giving details of how much urban poor groups spend on non-food needs.

York (UK 1899)*	1.67-2.33	9.9
Panama (1997)	1.74	15.3
Ethiopia (1995/96)	1.78	33.0
Nicaragua (1998)	1.9	30.5
Paraguay (1996)	2.0	39.5
Bolivia (1996)	2.0	64.5
Ecuador (1996)	2.0	55.2
Colombia (1996)	2.0	52.2
Mexico (1996)	2.0	20.5
Brazil (1996)	2.0	29.2
Kenya (1997)	2.1	49.0
Guatemala (2000)	2.26	27.1
Uruguay (1998)	2.75–3.1	24.7
USA (1960s)	3.0	

* This is drawn from B. Seebohm Rowntree's 1899 survey (Rowntree1902). The Engel coefficient varied according to the size of the family and the number of children; for instance, for families with two adults and 5 children it was 1.67; for single adults, it was 2.33.

N.B. The poverty line for Mauritania was not based on the cost of food but on a poverty line based on a US\$ 1 a day. There is considerable diversity between the nations listed above as to whether adjustments are made for differentials in costs between locations, on what basis the adjustments are made (in many documents this is not clear) and which locational categories are used (for instance 'rural' versus 'urban' or different geographic regions). See Annex 1 and 2 for more details and for sources.

The ways in which non-food requirements have been calculated are often arbitrary (see, for instance, Grootaert 1996, National Statistics Institute of Portugal 1999). In some instances, the allowance for non-food items is based on some multiple of the cost of a minimum food basket (the Engel coefficient), which is made only on the recognition that there are non-food items that need to be purchased to avoid poverty, but with no attempt to calculate how much is needed. The allowance for non-food needs may be based on the cost of a specified bundle of non-food items – in which case its appropriateness is dependent on the bundle being appropriate and the price data being accurate. Or it is based on what some defined set of poor households spend on non-food needs.

If it is based on the cost of specified non-food goods or on what a particular set of households spend on specified non-food goods, there are difficulties in knowing what non-food items are 'needs'; also on who should decide what should be included. Most allowances for non-food needs are ungenerous to the point of being unrealistic for urban contexts. An assessment of poverty in Kenya by the World Bank defined the absolute poverty line as "*…the minimum level of expenditure deemed necessary to satisfy a person's food requirements plus the consumption of a few non-food necessities*" (World Bank 1995). Most allowances rule out any expenditure on entertainment, cigarettes or alcohol. Expenditure on social obligations, such as weddings, dowries and funerals, also tends to fall outside the lists.[40]

Even expenditure on transport may not be considered a 'need' because this is considered not to meet a basic need directly but, rather, indirectly through access to needs such as work, education and health services. Deaton and Zaidi 2002 – which is a paper providing guidelines for constructing consumption aggregates from household survey data for setting poverty lines - acknowledge the problems faced by individuals who have high costs for 'regrettable necessities' (goods and services that yield no welfare in their own right but that have to be purchased), such as transport to work. They note how consumption expenditure for such individuals may overstate their welfare. However, they suggest that for those who have high transport to work costs, it is not possible to distinguish between those who cannot avoid these and those who can (for instance, those who choose to live in a pleasant suburb with high transport to work costs). So they suggest that no allowance should be made, while recognizing the 'occasional

---

[40] The exclusion of these is usually justified by pointing to the difficulty in determining how these affect income, because they are large but occasional expenditures.

injustice' in doing so. In many urban contexts, not allowing for transport costs in poverty lines is much more than an 'occasional injustice'.

The way in which allowances in poverty lines for non-food needs can be based on questionable assumptions is illustrated by Good's discussion of the setting of the poverty line for Botswana in 1991 (Good 1999). This reveals attitudes to 'the poor' that have much in common with how the Victorian middle classes viewed poverty in the United Kingdom during the 19th century. All measures were taken to keep poverty lines as low as possible. No allowance was made for children growing out of their clothes before they were worn out. There was no allowance for socks (except for school uniform), stockings, overcoats or waterproofs. There was no allocation for furniture, beds, mattresses, chairs or tables, except a bench so that "...*the head of household could discharge [his] social obligations towards an important visitor.*" Blankets and cooking pots were allowed, but their durability was emphasized, stressing that "...*with care some could last a lifetime.*" There was no allowance for forks, knives, spoons, candles, cups, etc. A poor person's health could be covered through two visits a year to a government clinic and one consultation 'with the traditional doctor'. No allowance was made for travelling (with a comment that the poor would have to walk if they were to seek work or attend social functions). And expenditure on alcohol or cigarettes was ruled out, as were sweets, soft drinks, snacks, toys, books or writing materials (Good 1999).

This example from Botswana may be an extreme one, but much of the literature on setting poverty lines has explicit comments about the need to keep any allowance for non-food costs to the minimum, or implicit assumptions about what 'poor' households deserve. The Poverty Reduction Strategy Paper for Zambia notes that the food basket used to arrive at the poverty line is very modest, and is based on a predominantly minimal calorific requirement that excluded meat, chicken and fish, and that the measurement "...has also not fully factored in such basic needs of the people as shelter, education, health care, lighting, clothing, footwear and transport" (Zambia, Republic of, 2002, page 22). In most poverty lines, there is also the assumption that the money available to a family is spent in the most rational way and only on 'needs' (for example, with nothing spent on entertainment or toys for children), and that there are no economic obligations beyond the basic nuclear family, including debt repayments (see, for instance, Wratten 1995 and Maxwell 1998).

Data problems, such as the lack of a recent household income or expenditure survey, may hamper the setting of any allowance in poverty lines for non-food needs. It is also difficult to define and measure the income needed for housing, unless it is rented (and data on rental levels can be obtained[41]), and for the acquisition of any durable good (Mozambique, Government of, Eduardo Mondlane University and IFPRI 1998).

The upward adjustment of poverty lines for non-food needs is now usually based on data on the expenditure by particular sets of 'low-income households' on non-food items. This avoids the difficulties noted above in defining 'the income needed for non-food needs'. Ravallion argues that the allowance for non-food needs should be anchored in the consumption behaviour of the poor (Ravallion 1998).

The two most common ways of doing this appear to be:
- The 'cost of basic needs' method, with the income that a household needs being based on the cost of a food basket, with allowance for non-food needs based on what households, whose *total expenditure* or *food expenditure* is equal to the food poverty line, spend on non-food items.
- The 'food-energy intake' method: a poverty line based on the lowest-income level at which households who appear to eat enough spend (on food and on non-food items). Ravallion 1998 notes the advantage of this, because of its relatively modest data requirements.

Where poverty lines are adjusted for the cost of non-food items (and many are not), most seem to use the first method above (see Annex 1). Most also base the allowance for non-food needs on what the poorest households spend on non-food items. For instance, reviewing the examples in Annex 1, allowance for non-food items is based on:

---

[41] Renters or tenants may be reluctant to say that they are paying rent, or to reveal how much they pay – see Weru 2004, for example.

- What the poor who are right on the food poverty line spend on non-food items (Cameroon, Ghana, Guatemala, Kenya, Malawi, Mongolia, Mozambique, Panama and Peru; also the lower poverty line in Bangladesh);
- What the poor whose expenditure on food is enough to meet their minimum food requirements spend on non-food items (Nepal; also the upper poverty line in Bangladesh)
- What the poorest 72 percent of rural households spend on non-food items in Haiti;
- What the poorest 25 percent of the population spend on non-food items in Tanzania; and
- The proportion of income spent on non-food items by the second poorest decile in Uruguay.

If the allowance for non-food needs is based on what a specified reference group spends on non-food items, the size of this allowance is greatly influenced by which reference group is chosen – for instance, those whose total expenditure is at the food poverty line, the poorest 10 percent, 20 percent or poorest half of the total population.[42] In Uruguay, if the first decile had been used rather than the second decile, the poverty line would have been some 25 percent lower (World Bank 2001a).

It is perhaps worth noting that when the US government first set an income-based poverty line in the early 1960s, it based the allowance for non-food needs on the proportion of household income spent on non-food items for the whole US population (Citro and Michael 1995). This led to a poverty line set at three times the cost of a 'minimum food basket' – which is notably higher than virtually all the poverty lines used in low- and middle-income nations today. Even in the first recorded use of an income-based poverty line – by Rowntree in the city of York in Victorian England in a study in 1899 – the poverty line was set much higher than for most nations today. Rowntree also stressed that the poverty line used was set very low and that those below it had insufficient to obtain 'the minimum necessaries for the maintenance of physical efficiency.' The poverty line was set at 2.33 times the cost of a minimum food food basket for single adults and between 1.67 and 1.76 for households with two adults and one or more child (Rowntree 1902).

There seems to be little questioning of the validity of basing the allowance for 'non-food' needs on the non-food expenditure of the groups likely to have the least adequate provision for non-food needs. What poor groups spend on non-food items is not a measure of the income needed to afford essential non-food items, but simply the expenditure by a particular set of low-income households on non-food items, regardless of whether their needs are met. This is especially so if the allowance for non-food needs is based on the non-food expenditure of households whose *total* income is just sufficient to afford minimum food requirements. As Mearns (2004) notes, this implies that individuals or households with below poverty line incomes will have to remain under-nourished if they are to afford non-food needs. So the reference group for defining how much households are allowed for non-food needs within poverty lines are those who are guaranteed not to have enough for non-food needs.

A survey in Mozambique in 1997 recognized that it would be better to base the allowance for non-food needs on what is spent on these by households whose food expenditure was the cost of the minimum food basket. But this would have qualified virtually everyone in Mozambique as poor – so setting a poverty line based on this would not help identify those who were particularly poor (Government of Mozambique, Eduardo Mondlane University and IFPRI 1998).

Considerable care is needed in drawing on data on what low-income groups (or food-poor groups) spend on non-food items as a basis for defining what is needed for urban households. Their non-food expenditure is often simply an indication of the high cost of inadequate provision. It is not appropriate to base what low-income households need for housing, schooling and health care on what they spend on these, when these same households cannot afford to spend enough to get adequate housing, health care and schooling for their children. For instance, setting allowances for housing costs within poverty lines based on what a particular set of 'low-income households' spend on housing often means allocating only enough for low-income households to afford very inadequate quality accommodation – for instance, whole households living in one-room shacks made of temporary materials, that they constructed themselves on land sites that are insecure, dangerous and poorly located with regard to income-earning

---

[42] See Grootaert 1996 for a discussion of this with regard to the Côte d'Ivoire.

opportunities, with very inadequate or no provision for water, sanitation and drainage. A low-income family that is paying 20 percent of its income to rent a tiny room with no piped water supply and no sanitation facility, and another 10 percent on water purchased from a vendor (but with the water costs too high to allow them to buy enough to meet household needs) is not avoiding deprivation by spending 30 percent of its income on these. It may need to spend the equivalent of 60 or more percent of its income to get adequate quality accommodation with adequate provision for water and sanitation, but it cannot do so because other costs have to be met (food, keeping children at school, transport fares to and from work and services.....). The extent to which large sections of the population in most cities in Africa, Asia and Latin America live in conditions such as these has been documented for many years,[43] but this has been all but ignored by most discussions of how to set poverty lines. In most cities, what poorer groups spend on housing is a very inadequate basis for estimating what income they need to get reasonable quality housing. Poverty lines can even be set so low that a significant proportion of homeless people are not classified as 'poor'.[44]

Expenditure data showing low expenditure on food or non-food essentials may be the result of poor groups going without – for instance, cutting back on essential food expenditures to keep children at school (see Mupedziswa and Gumbo 1998) or not seeking treatment for illness or injury (which, in expenditure data, could be interpreted as not needing to spend much on health care). They may be spending less on education because their children do not go to school, and spending less on housing because they live in the streets or squat; see, for instance, the analysis of expenditures by urban households in Dhaka who have below poverty line incomes, which shows that the poorest groups (with incomes of less than 43 percent of the poverty line income) spent a lower proportion of their incomes on housing and education than those whose incomes were 43–100 percent of the poverty line (Islam, Huda, Narayan et al 1997). Poor groups often spend less on water by using dirty, contaminated water for most of their household needs. Poor households who have no toilet in their home often spend less on using pay-toilets, by defecating in the open. They often spend less on transport because they walk very long distances to and from work or services and shops.

Many of the studies on whose data the Engel coefficient is calculated draw on national or rural expenditure data, not on expenditure data for individual cities. A relatively small change in the Engel coefficient can have a large impact on the poverty line (Mejía and Vos 1997). If the calculation of the income required for non-food needs is based on national data on household expenditure, it will under-estimate the income needed in locations where non-food needs are particularly costly, which is likely to be mainly in the larger and/or more prosperous cities. The high proportion of income being spent by sections of the urban populations on housing and on other non-food needs is discussed in more detail in Section IV.

c. Equivalence scales

One final issue to consider in relation to the way consumption-based poverty lines may under-state (or over-state) the scale and depth of poverty is whether equivalence scales are used to adjust household data to produce statistics for the proportion of people who are poor, and how these scales are used. Often, the unit for expenditure or income data is the household, but most statistics on poverty refer to individual status (Grewe and Becker 2001). In these cases, the household data must be scaled down to represent an individual. When the literature does not ignore the problem of accounting for the effect of household size on expenditure, it is not always immediately apparent how particular authors have adjusted their data to handle this problem (ibid).

---

[43] For reviews, see WHO 1992, UNCHS 1996, Hardoy, Mitlin and Satterthwaite 2001; but see also this documentation back into the 1960s and 1970s, including Abrams 1964, Ward 1976, Turner 1976....).

[44] See Swaminathan 1995, which reports on different estimates for the proportion of 'slum' households and 'pavement dwellers' in Mumbai who have below poverty line incomes; the main surprise is that 30–45 percent of pavement dwellers are reported to have incomes above the income poverty line for surveys taken during the 1970s and 1980s. This could be taken as a confirmation that many non-poor households live on the pavements – but given the very poor conditions, the insecurity and the lack of basic services for those who dwell on the pavements (ibid, SPARC 1988), the lack of provision for non-food needs when setting poverty lines and the high cost of housing in Mumbai are more likely.

Many governments ignore differences in household size and in the number of dependants, although there is some evidence suggesting that adjustments for household size can make a significant difference to poverty estimates (Grewe and Becker 2001). The differences in the incomes needed to avoid poverty between households of different sizes and compositions (infants, young children, adults of working age, non-working adults including those who have retired…) are sometimes taken into account by using 'equivalence scales', which may either be imposed externally or constructed statistically from survey data. The use of equivalence scales is thus to adjust for demographic differences in the household. There have also been attempts to recognize the existence of economies of scale in the household – for instance, feeding and housing six people and providing consumer durables is not six times more expensive than feeding and housing one person (see, for instance, Deaton and Zaidi 2002).

Setting accurate equivalence scales is difficult, even in high-income nations with much richer and more detailed data available. A detailed review on measuring poverty in the USA noted the lack of agreement on how equivalence scales should be calculated, and that many different scales are found which have "…*very different implications for the total number of people in poverty as well as the distribution of poverty among families of different types*" (Citro and Michael 1995, page 160). Where equivalence scales are used, most studies in low- and middle-income countries have been restricted to studying the scale parameters only for food items (Deaton and Paxson 1995). By doing so, they may give inadequate attention to non-food costs – for instance, for children.

Equivalence scales assume that children under 18 consume less than adults (and so need less income to ensure their consumption needs are met), so poverty lines for households with children are adjusted downwards, using an equivalence scale. The recommended scale of this downward adjustment can be large. For instance, Deaton and Zaidi 2002 note: "Most of the literature – as well as common sense – suggests that children are relatively more expensive in industrialized countries (school fees, entertainment, clothes etc) and relatively cheap in poorer agricultural economies" (page 52). They suggest that the cost of each child is close to the cost of each adult in US and Western Europe and perhaps as low as 0.25 or 0.3 of the cost of each adult for the poorest economies. But whether or not children are so much cheaper than adults (and by how much) depends on many factors, such as the cost of keeping children at school, whether day care has to be paid for to allow one or more adult to increase their income-earning possibilities, the cost of getting children treatment and medicines when they are sick (and how often they are in need of treatment and medicines), the cost of keeping them clothed and with shoes that fit as they grow….. Also, small children are unable to consume the quantities of low-nutrient foods necessary to meet their growth needs and is their need for more nutritious (and generally more expensive) food considered when setting equivalence scales?

Perhaps equivalence scales developed in nations where children have free access to schools (and where associated costs such as stationery, text books, exam fees, school lunches, transport to and from school are also provided free) and free access to health services (and free or subsidized medicines) are being applied in nations where none of these are available to low-income households. For those living in poor quality homes with inadequate provision for water, sanitation, drainage and garbage removal, infants and children are likely to need more frequent visits to health services and more medicines, and this can be expensive. There is also the cost from the loss of income when working adults have to stay at home to nurse sick children. All this may make children who go to school and who can visit health services and get medicines when they are sick as costly as adults, or at least more costly than the equivalence scales assume.

d. Extreme poverty lines

As the poverty definitions listed in Annex 1 illustrate, most governments set lower poverty lines that claim to measure 'extreme poverty' and that are based only on the cost of a minimum food basket. Virtually all the nations listed in Annex 1 use an extreme poverty line, while some set this as the only poverty line (which implies that it is valid to measure poverty based on income levels that make no allowance for non-food expenditure). In most urban contexts, where access to virtually all needs is monetized, this should be recognized as having no validity, unless an extreme poverty line is used to ensure that those facing 'extreme poverty' get the necessary support to allow them to meet their nutritional requirements, and its limitations are recognized. Yet it is still common for documents on poverty to stress how the proportion of the population in 'extreme poverty' is much higher in rural areas than in urban areas. This is often stated with no explicit recognition of the higher income needed to avoid poverty (including paying for many non-food needs) in many urban areas.

If we were to take infant and child mortality rates as an indicator with some validity in indicating extreme poverty, in many sub-Saharan African nations, the differences in such mortality rates between rural and urban areas appear to be much less than the discourse, which emphasizes how the proportion of the population suffering from extreme poverty is much higher in rural areas than in urban areas.[45]

This use of an extreme poverty line has more validity if and when those who are found to fall below this poverty line have guaranteed access to (for instance) accommodation that has adequate provision for water and sanitation, and also to health care and schools. The idea of having this lower poverty line measuring extreme poverty based only on the income needed to afford an adequate food basket had more validity in European high-income countries at a time when access to health care, education (and often child care or nursery schools) was free, where virtually all housing had adequate provision for water, sanitation and drainage, and where there were additional welfare measures that sought to find accommodation for those with below poverty line incomes or sought to cover their housing costs. But, as Beck 1994 notes, this concept has been transferred uncritically to nations where few if any of these conditions are present.

e. How ineffective local governance increases non-food costs

Where local government institutions are too weak, ineffective or unrepresentative to ensure provision of basic infrastructure and services, the gap between official poverty lines and the income needed to avoid living in poverty can be particularly high. The term governance is used because it encompasses both the performance of government institutions (political, bureaucratic, legislative) and the nature and quality of their relationships with civil society actors (including citizens, community organizations and NGOs). Local government responsibilities for infrastructure and service provision may be realized through support for private and community provision – and provision in partnership with urban poor organizations often allows under-resourced local authorities to considerably increase the scale and effectiveness of their impact (a point to which we will return in Sections VII and VIII).

As discussed in more detail in Section IV, studies of the expenditures of low-income urban households show that many face particularly high costs for many non-food essentials – typically on water from vendors, sanitation from pay-as-you-use facilities, health care and medicines (especially where there are no government or non-profit services), housing rent or the cost of land and self-build, schools (especially where government provision is poor) and public transport (especially where low-income groups choose peripheral/distant locations because the land is cheaper and/or households have more chance of developing their own homes without fear of eviction).

This also means that more effective local governance can reduce these costs, so it can reduce poverty without increasing incomes because non-food costs are reduced or better living conditions are provided with no increase in cost. Most urban settings also provide economies of scale and proximity for infrastructure and services, which should reduce the gap between good quality provision and what poor households can afford to pay – as will be discussed in more detail later.

Thus, in most urban contexts, whether or not a household is above or below a consumption-based poverty line may have little bearing on their capacity to get access to many essential goods or services. In most urban contexts, access to these is influenced by many other factors, including the quality of local governance, and individual or household factors such as whether the household has a legal address, their educational level, the information available to them, their legal rights (and whether there are provisions to ensure these are respected), gender (including, in many locations, constraints on the possibilities for women to obtain land for housing, credit, house ownership….) and political affiliations.

---

[45] See Annex 3 for comparisons of infant and child mortality rates between rural and urban areas.

f. Little or no adjustment for variations in prices within nations

Where a poverty line is used, whether based on price or consumption data, *it has little validity unless it accurately reflects the income level that an individual or household needs to avoid poverty in their particular neighbourhood (whether it is a village, small town, city or large metropolis).* The income level needed to avoid poverty is likely to vary considerably between different locations within nations. It is likely to be particularly high in larger and/or more prosperous urban centres. It may be that price differences between locations for some essentials goods and services are unusually high in some low- and middle-income countries because of the large differences between locations in the extent to which access to these goods and services is monetized and the extent to which the local economy is incorporated into wider regional, national or global economies. For instance, there are likely to be very large differences in the price of the cheapest reasonable quality, secure, legal shelter in India between, say, Mumbai and most small urban centres that serve primarily as administrative centres within poor farming regions where much production is still subsistence. One would expect large differences in the price of reasonable quality, secure, legal shelters in sub-Saharan Africa between national capitals and most small urban centres in low-income regions. It is likely that the price of the cheapest reasonable quality accommodation relative to local incomes will be particularly high, the more inadequate the quality of local governance with regard to provision for infrastructure and services and a regulatory framework for land for housing. Obviously, the price of all housing with infrastructure and services is influenced by the quality and extent of infrastructure and service provision; where provision lags far behind need and demand, the price of housing with adequate provision becomes inflated. The price of the cheapest legal house can be much increased by expensive and slow official regulatory frameworks to approve land sub-divisions and by unnecessarily large minimum plot sizes.

The need for poverty lines to be adjusted so that they reflect the real costs of food and non-food essentials in each location is widely acknowledged in the poverty literature (see, for instance, Montgomery, Stren, Cohen and Reed 2003), yet many governments and international agencies still disregard this when setting poverty lines; in Annex 1, ten poverty lines are used with no allowance made for spatial differences. These are among the many nations that still have the same poverty line applied throughout the national territory; this assumes that the income needed to avoid poverty is the same in all locations within the national territory, from the largest and most prosperous cities to small rural settlements. This is changing, as an increasing number of nations make some adjustment – typically, an upward adjustment of the poverty line 'for urban areas' (see Annex 1). If the poverty definitions used in recent poverty assessments or Poverty Reduction Strategy Papers (summarized in Annex 1) are compared to the definitions listed in Tabatabai with Fouad 1993, it appears that many more nations are making adjustments for regional variations than in the 1980s or early 1990s. A poverty assessment for Togo notes that: "*When applied to a country with considerable regional variation, overall poverty lines can become meaningless. In Togo, setting a single national poverty line that is applied to the population as a whole results in significant over-estimates of the number of poor households in rural communities compared to urban communities, particularly in the north*" (Annex 1, page 5).

But a general adjustment 'for urban areas' still misses the fact that, in most nations, there are likely to be large differences between urban centres, so this may still under-state income poverty in the urban locations where prices are particularly high.[46] It might overstate income poverty in some of the poorer (and generally smaller) urban centres. In addition, it may be that the adjustments for spatial variations in the cost of living are based on food prices when the spatial variation in the cost of non-food items is greater (Hentschel and Lanjouw 1996).

Annex 1 gives details of whether provision was made for spatial variations in the income needed to avoid poverty when setting poverty lines. For those nations in which such provision was made, this can be in the form of adjustments by geographic regions/provinces/states, adjustments between urban and rural, or a combination of the two. In some, there is simply an adjustment for all urban areas – for instance, in

---

[46] In the USA, adjusting for housing costs alone would significantly shift the US poverty profile, with the likely effect of raising estimates of poverty in metropolitan areas (Citro and Michael 1995); it may be that locational cost-of-living adjustments in low- and middle-income countries would need to be larger than in the USA because living costs for poorer groups are increased by poor governance, as discussed in a later section of this paper.

Ethiopia and Kenya; in others, adjustment is made for more than this (for instance, for the capital or largest city, 'other urban centres' and rural areas, as in the Gambia and Tanzania). In Yemen, poverty lines were adjusted both regionally (governorates) and between rural and urban areas although, unusually, rural poverty lines were set slightly higher than urban poverty lines (presumably because they were based on food expenditure, with an assumption that activity levels were higher in rural areas, so rural populations needed more calories per person).[47]

Of course, the appropriateness of the allowances made for spatial variations in poverty lines depends on whether these can actually measure the spatial differences in the income levels needed to avoid poverty. For instance, there may be little data available on non-food prices, or all the data that are available are for non-food items sold in shops or markets, and so no account is taken of the spatial variations in spending on items such as transport, health care, water bills, housing and keeping children in school.

Perhaps the most astonishing gap revealed by the review of the literature on which this paper draws is the lack of any study that examined how much income would be needed in particular locations to allow an individual or household to avoid poverty. It would be revealing to see for different locations at what income level households would typically be able to afford sufficient food, a legal, reasonable quality house with adequate provision for water, sanitation and electricity (and the utility bills these entail), keep their children at school and afford health care and treatment for those who are sick. It is likely that the income needed to afford this would be far above official poverty lines in many urban locations in most nations.

In discussing the adjustments to poverty lines needed to allow for differences between locations, there may be an assumption that urban poverty is over-stated rather than under-stated. For instance, the discussion on the use of the food-energy intake method in Ravallion 1998 suggests that this is likely to: over-state urban poverty, because urban dwellers may spend more on food because non-food items are cheaper; have lower activity levels and so need less food; have different tastes and spend more per calorie (so it is choice not need that makes them spend more on food); have lower prices for other goods and services; and consume a diet that is nutritionally better balanced because of better access to health care and schooling (see Ravallion 1998). But it can also be suggested that urban households spend more on food (or pay more per calorie) because of constraints on time to cook or prepare food, or the high cost of fuel; that many groups within the urban labour force have very high activity levels (which Ravallion acknowledges); and that significant sections of the urban population face higher costs for many non-food necessities (discussed in more detail in a later section). Deaton and Tarozzi 2000 suggest that urban poverty is over-stated in India because the urban poverty line is set too high – but, as the authors admit, the rural and urban poverty lines omitted the prices of housing and of transport.[48] For many urban poor households (especially those living in the larger or more prosperous cities), these are major costs (or, if they are not, it is because they have such inadequate provision e.g. living on the pavements). This is an issue discussed in more detail in Section IV

International agencies may not acknowledge the need for adjustments in poverty lines within nations to reflect spatial variations in the income needed to avoid poverty, but they do acknowledge very large differences in the cost of living within these same nations for their own staff, as the daily 'per diems' they receive to cover their living costs are adjusted by location. Within most low- and middle-income nations, the daily rate that international agency staff receive to pay for hotels and for 'other costs' varies

---

[47] For discussions of how allowance was made for spatial variations in costs, see Datt and Jolliffe 1999 for Egypt, Grootaert 1996 for Côte d'Ivoire, Mozambique, Government of, Eduardo Mondlane University and IFPRI 1998 for Mozambique and Lanjouw, Prennushi and Zaidi 1999.

[48] Deaton and Tarozzi 2000 list the 228 commodities for which expenditure data is collected in India's National Sample Survey, 50th round. It shows the careful and detailed attention given to food expenditures (most items are food items) and to fuel expenditures (all non-food items are for fuel/energy). By implication, 'the poor' only need food and fuel. This is not an appropriate basis for gauging the income that poor households need in locations where many other needs are monetized and where the cost of meeting these needs would represent a significant proportion of the income for low-income households (and often more than they can afford, so these non-food and fuel needs are not met).

by a factor of 2–4, depending on whether they stay in capital cities or other high-price cities, lower-price urban centres or rural areas; in some nations, the variation is much higher than this – see Table 2.

Table 2: Intra-national variations in the per diems paid to international staff to cover their living costs

Nation	Variation between locations in daily subsistence allowance, including hotel (US$)	Variation between locations in daily subsistence allowance not including hotel (US $)
Angola	103–229	58–99
Argentina	60–158	28–41
Bangladesh	38–187	18–67
Bolivia	45–132	11–42
Brazil	46–150	17–59
Burundi	17–193	13–73
Cambodia	27–177	13–62
Chad	59–215	26–95
Colombia	41–126	13–40
Côte d'Ivoire	42–212	23–85
Ethiopia	39–235	17–92
Ghana	59–199	29–76
Kenya	56–200	24–72
Lesotho	56–110	29–30
Malaysia	30–118	12–57
Mexico	93–252	42–88
Mozambique	68–165	34–74
Namibia	25–90	13–32
Uganda	37–209	16–54
Venezuela	77–213	36–81
Zambia	44–170	22–66
Zimbabwe	51–160	11–66

Drawn from the UN web site, based on April 2003 rates. There are a few exceptions that fall outside these ranges – for instance, where a hotel rate includes all meals.

Table 2 also includes the figures for the daily allowance independent of the hotel bill, and these vary by a factor of 2–3 for most nations and 4–5 for some. Thus, relatively sophisticated measures are taken to guarantee that international agency staff and international consultants have their 'daily cost of living' adjusted to meet the differences in costs between locations within nations – but little or no such recognition is accorded to 'the poor' in setting poverty lines.

g. Little adjustment for variations in costs or prices between nations

The price of most essential goods and services is also likely to vary considerably between countries; in general, the monetary income required for most non-food essentials in urban areas is likely to be higher in the more urbanized middle-income nations than in the less urbanized low-income nations.[49] Yet, the use of the same income-based poverty line for all nations (adjusted for purchasing power parity) is being promoted, and the US$1 a day poverty line is the main indicator of poverty being used within the Millennium Development Goals.

Although the Poverty Reduction Strategy Papers that most nations have developed in collaboration with external donors (including the World Bank) do not use the US$1 a day poverty line or, if they do,

---

[49] As discussed later, the quality and availability of education, health care, piped water, good quality sanitation, and drainage and garbage collection is generally better in middle-income nations than low-income nations; where there are competent, effective and accountable urban governments (which are more common in middle-income nations), these may bring both benefits and lower prices for large sections of the urban poor.

consideration is also given to nationally set poverty lines, the World Bank still uses the US$1 a day poverty line in much of its general literature. The US$1 per person per day poverty line implies that the income needed to avoid poverty does not vary within nations or between nations (when calculated in dollars with purchasing power parity). This assumes that the income needed to avoid poverty is the same in cities such as Buenos Aires, Caracas, São Paulo and Mexico City – large cities where access to all goods and services is highly monetized and where access for many poorer groups is particularly expensive – as it is in the small urban centres in sub-Saharan Africa and Asia, in regions with very low average per capita incomes and where much of the economy is based on self-production or barter. If the US$1 a day poverty line is valid for all low- and middle-income nations, then why is it not valid also for high-income nations? But to suggest that a US$1 per person per day is all that an individual or household requires to cover needs for food, accommodation, utility bills, health care, keeping children at school and transport in New York, London or Tokyo is clearly ridiculous. One wonders whether it has much validity in most large cities in most middle-income and many low-income nations. Does a dollar per person per day really allow an individual or a household to avoid poverty in São Paulo or Mexico City – or in major cities in nations with much lower per capita incomes than Brazil or Mexico, such as Delhi and Mumbai in India or Nairobi in Kenya? In some cities, US$1 a day would be unlikely to cover the cost that many low-income earners face going to and from work; for some low-income communities, it would hardly cover the cost of water that has to be purchased from water vendors, and would certainly not be enough to purchase the volume of water that households need.[50]

But for international agencies, the attraction of using a single measure to capture and compare situations between different national and regional settings remains. Ravallion and Bidani 1994 highlight the pros and cons of using a consistent poverty line that reflects 'local' (by which they mean national) perceptions of what constitutes poverty (referred to as *specificity*). Using national perceptions would mean that two households deemed to have the same standard of living could not be said to both be either above or below the poverty line. Ravallion and Bidani 1994 illustrate this by noting how the use of nationally set poverty lines can have 'absurd' policy implications, as in comparing the incidence of poverty between Indonesia and the USA. In 1990, both estimates for poverty incidence were at about the same level, at 14–15 percent of the population, but there are clearly more people in Indonesia who would be deemed poor than in the United States (Ravallion and Bidani 1994). But one wonders what the absurd policy implications of this actually are (official discussions in Indonesia about setting the poverty line are hardly likely to be influenced by poverty levels in the USA). It is likely that the policy implications of using the US$1 a day poverty line are more absurd, especially for the poor who live in the worst governed and most expensive cities.

IV. COSTS FOR NON-FOOD ESSENTIALS

a. The high proportion of income spent by low-income urban groups on non-food essentials

Many empirical studies show the high costs paid by particular urban groups (or those living in particular settlements within urban centres) for non-food essentials, or the high proportion of their income that goes on these – and this section gives many examples of this. These raise questions about the validity of poverty lines that make no allowance for non-food items, or poverty lines that are set on the assumption that non-food items require only a small proportion of income. They should serve as a caution for poverty lines that draw on price or expenditure data, in that they highlight how particular (urban) groups are paying or spending well above any 'average' and also highlight the importance of ensuring representative samples. They also highlight the high prices paid by many low-income urban households for housing and for transport, and these are items that may not be included in defining poverty lines.

Most household expenditure surveys show urban populations or particular groups within the urban population spending an above-average proportion of their incomes on housing and transport.[51] It would

---

[50] Many low-income households do have to purchase water from vendors that is very expensive per unit volume. When the water is expensive, they will generally use cheaper but less readily available and worse quality water sources for most household tasks; see UN Habitat 2003a.

[51] This may not indicate that these are more expensive in urban areas but, rather, that urban households or urban

also be surprising if costs such as housing and transport to and from work were not generally more expensive in urban areas than in rural areas. In most urban contexts, access to housing (to rent), land for housing (to rent or own) and building materials (for building a house) are all monetized, whereas in many rural contexts, they are not. Access to permission to build a house is also generally monetized in urban areas (or in the more important urban centres), and this can be costly (for instance, in time and professional fees or through the informal payments that have to be made). Similarly, for transport, it is likely that large sections of the low-income urban population face higher costs for transport than most of the rural population because they live in locations at some distance from places where they earn incomes or where services are available. The best locations in urban areas are relatively costly, including those with good access to employment and services, so many low-income households choose peripheral locations because accommodation is cheaper (or the possibilities of avoiding high rental costs and of owner-occupation and self-build are greater). It is also likely that the larger and more prosperous the urban centre, the larger the rural:urban differences in the prices paid by poorer groups for housing and land for housing and in the costs of transport.[52]

This is not to claim that housing or transport costs are always higher in urban areas than in rural areas; agricultural labourers or temporary farm workers may be paying significant proportions of their income to rent (usually very poor quality) accommodation, and face particularly high costs for many essential commodities. A comparison of how much rural and urban dwellers spend on transport also does not take into account what (rural and urban) households forgo because transport is too costly or not available – and obviously, rural disadvantages in this regard are generally much greater than urban disadvantages. Urban dwellers will generally benefit from cheaper manufactured goods than rural dwellers – and the larger and better located the urban area, the larger this benefit is likely to be. The same is true for many services.

However, with these reservations in mind, it is worth noting the empirical studies that show the particularly high cost for non-food essentials paid by urban populations or by particular urban groups, or the high proportion of incomes that goes on these.

(a) *Public transport* (for getting to and from work and essential services). Various studies of urban poor communities show that public transport costs represent a significant part of total household expenditure (see, for instance, URC 2001; also Grootaert 1996 for Côte d'Ivoire in general). In Zambia, an analysis of household expenditure for urban populations found that 12 percent was spent on transport (Central Statistical Office, Zambia 1997);[53] in Malawi, an analysis of household expenditure in four cities found that transport costs represented 12.5–14 percent of total expenditure (Malawi, Government of, 1994). Expenditures are likely to be particularly high for poorer groups who live on city peripheries because only here could they find land sites on which they could build housing.

---

poor households choose to spend more on them although, in most instances, urban poor households' expenditures on these are more likely to be related to need rather than choice. This section's focus is on whether sufficient allowance is made in poverty lines for non-food costs for urban populations, not about whether non-food costs are higher in urban areas than in rural areas. Some non-food costs are likely to be higher in rural areas than in urban areas; income-based poverty measures also fail to highlight some serious rural deprivations, such as access to services and (producer and consumer) markets. However, some discussion of rural–urban differences in non-food costs is necessary if poverty lines use national or rural household survey data to calculate non-food needs, and so make little or no allowance for those non-food items that are generally more expensive in urban areas (or particular urban centres or districts).

[52] There are few empirical studies of poverty in small urban centres, even though a substantial proportion of the urban population in virtually all nations lives in small urban centres. These include many urban centres with a few thousand inhabitants. In many small urban centres and in some larger urban centres (or urban districts within larger urban centres) in low-income regions, access to land for housing and materials for building may be less monetized, and there may be few or no administrative controls that limit supplies (and increase costs). There are also likely to be many rural areas where markets for housing and for the components of housing (and permission to build) are also monetized – including rural areas that become desired locations for higher-income groups (for instance, for tourism or second homes or homes from which they commute to urban areas) or non-agricultural enterprises.

[53] Despite evidence that a high share of household expenditures in urban areas goes on non-food items such as transport and housing, the poverty line was still set at only 1.3 times the cost of a basic food basket.

(b) *Education* (including school fees and associated costs, including getting to and from school). Devas and Korboe 2000 note the difficulties that poor urban households in Kumasi face in affording the fees for primary schools and additional costs (unofficial fees, transport, examination fees, textbooks and uniforms). Even where entry to schools is free, there may be other costs such as the cost of uniforms, school meals or exam fees, which make it expensive for poor urban households to keep their children at school (as an example, see Kanji 1995 who discusses this for a settlement in Harare).[54]

Some of the evidence for the high cost of keeping children at school is for national averages, not for urban areas or for particular cities. A poverty profile for the Cameroon notes how much households spend on keeping their children at school – including expenditure on materials and supplies (books, notebooks, uniforms, other materials and school supplies), fees (for tuition, parent–teacher associations, room and board, rehearsals, exams, registration), and other materials and education fees such as home instruction, school lunches and transport (Cameroon, Republic of, 2002). Kwon 1998 and Lee 1998 note the high proportion of income spent by many low-income households in South Korea on education. A poverty assessment in Kenya noted how a sizeable proportion of the expenditure of poor households was on education (Kenya, Government of, 2000). In other instances, the evidence is from urban areas. In a survey of four Indian cities (Baroda, Bhilwara, Sambalpur and Siliguri), Ghosh, Ahmad and Maitra 1994 found that the expenditure of low-income households on education (including fees, books and uniform) ranged from 4.8 to 15.6 percent of household income in the different cities. Bigsten and Kayizzi-Mugerwa 1992 found that a high proportion of the income of the poorest quintiles in Kampala was spent on educational services. A study of poverty in the Ivory Coast (Côte d'Ivoire, République de, 2000) showed a sharp increase in the proportion of urban household expenditure going on education between 1993 and 1998 (from 1.8 to 5.8 percent[55]), and comparable increases may have been common in many other nations as charges for education were introduced or increased during the 1990s. The study in Kenya noted above also emphasized how high the expenditure on education was among the urban poor, especially for secondary education. It also gave further evidence of the point noted above for other urban centres – that even if primary schools are free, there are still many expenses that have to be met to keep children there, such as uniforms, payment for watchmen and contributions to school supplies (Kenya, Government of, 2000). Low-income groups may also have to bear the cost of sending their children to 'private' schools because they cannot get places at government schools. The Pakistan NGO, Orangi Pilot Project, found that in Orangi, Karachi's largest informal settlement (with around a million inhabitants), a high proportion of the population sent their children to private schools because there were so few government schools (Orangi Pilot Project 1995).

(c) *Housing.* Most low-income households in urban areas spend a significant proportion of their income on housing and on the services associated with it (such as water, sanitation, electricity and solid waste collection). But it is difficult to ascertain what proportion of income is spent on this because of the many different ways in which these costs manifest themselves and are paid. For instance, for tenants or lodgers, these costs may take the form of regular rent payments – but getting rental accommodation may also require a one-off payment or a large deposit.[56]

Much of the low-income population in urban areas in low- and middle-income nations live in houses or shacks whose construction was organized by their occupiers.[57] For those living in a self-built house, payments may arise from getting the land site for the house. It may be assumed that those who live in illegal settlements as *de facto* owner-occupiers obtained the land free – but many illegal settlements are illegal sub-divisions rather than illegal occupations, so the land site had to be purchased, even if its development for housing was not approved by the relevant government authority. In addition, even in squatter settlements, many households may have 'purchased' the site from the original occupier or had to

---

[54] Kanji 1995 also documented how, in Zimbabwe in 1992, primary school fees were introduced in urban areas but not in rural areas, and how fees for secondary schools were higher in urban areas than in rural areas. Devas and Korboe 2000 note how charges had been introduced in Ghana for health and education.

[55] The proportion of total expenditure going to education also increased in rural areas – from 0.8 to 2.8 percent.

[56] Hardoy and Satterthwaite 1989; see also Beijaard 1995.

[57] This is hardly ever acknowledged in the general literature on poverty – although it has been one of the main themes of the literature on urban development from the 1960s onwards – see Abrams 1964, Turner 1976, Ward 1976, Hardoy and Satterthwaite 1989, UNCHS 1996, UN-Habitat 2003b.

make informal payments to local politicians, civil servants or local leaders.[58] Even where land sites for housing are allocated by government rather than by market mechanisms, it cannot be assumed that the poor benefit or that they get the land free (see, for instance, Kironde 1995 discussing this for Dar es Salaam).

For those who are building their own homes, there are also the costs of building, extending and maintaining the house, including the cost of building materials and fixtures – and, where needed, payment to those employed to undertake part of this work. Maintaining poor quality housing is often expensive and requires expenditure each year, but this would not considered part of 'non-food needs' in most poverty line calculations. Many low-income households who acquire or build their own houses and who take out a loan to help finance these (or to pay for the land sites) may also be paying a significant proportion of their incomes on loan repayments.

Owner-occupiers may face other costs that are expensive – for instance building permits or connection fees for piped water, sewers or electricity or land registration costs. Households seeking land for housing from local authorities may have to pay each year to remain on the housing list. Many sources acknowledge the difficulty of getting appropriate data on housing costs (especially for owner-occupiers). Deaton and Zaidi (2002) note that :"Of all the components of the household consumption aggregate, the housing sub-aggregate is often one of the most problematic" (page 37). It is likely that most poverty lines make inadequate allowance for the income needed for housing in the locations where housing is particularly expensive (mainly the larger and more prosperous cities) because of:

- inappropriate assumptions (for instance, the assumption that 'owner occupiers' face no housing costs or that what low-income households spend on housing is what they need to meet their housing needs); or
- the application of an average-figure for 'the income needed for housing' for all locations (when there are large variations in housing costs within the nation).

In Dhaka, in 1995, 11 percent of expenditure in households with below poverty line incomes went on housing (Islam, Huda, Narayan et al 1997). In Maputo City (Mozambique) in 1996/97, 17.7 percent of average household expenditure was housing-related (official government statistics quoted in Jenkins 2000). Expenditure surveys in Honduras and Kenya highlighted the high proportion of expenditure going on rents in urban areas (World Bank 2001b, Kenya, Government of, 2000); in Kenya, among the urban poor, it was the largest single expenditure on non-food items (ibid). But such averages can hide the high proportion of income spent by many low-income tenants. These 'averages' are brought down by those urban dwellers who squat; a significant proportion of low-income groups have expenditures on rent that are much higher than the average. For instance, in Dhaka, many poorer groups have expenditures of more than 11 percent of their income on housing (Islam, Huda, Narayan et al 1997). Various studies in other cities show that many tenant households spend more than one-quarter of their income on rent.[59] In South Korea, it is not unusual for poor households to pay one-quarter of their monthly income on rent (Asian Coalition for Housing Rights 1989, Lee 1998). Rakodi and Withers 1995 show how the lowest-income group of lodgers in the high-density areas in Harare and Gweru had a much higher proportion of their income going on housing (39 percent in Harare, 46 percent in Gweru) than other groups. It is also worth noting that land invasions by low-income households have often been driven by households seeking to escape high rental costs; in the large-scale land invasions that took place in Buenos Aires in 1982, many of the households were moving from rental accommodation whose costs they were having great difficulty affording.[60]

---

[58] See, for instance, Hasan 1999 for Karachi and Yapi-Diahou 1995 for Abidjan.

[59] See, for instance, Barbosa, Cabannes and Moraes 1997, Richmond 1997, UNCHS and World Bank 1993, UNCHS 1993, UNDP 1998 and Rakodi and Withers 1995. It is worth noting that rent accounted for 17-21 percent of the 'poverty-line income' that Rowntree calculated was necessary for minimum necessities in York in 1899 (Rowntree 1902). The allowance for rent varied, according to the size of the household.

[60] Of course, many other local factors were also present, including the rent increases that had taken place because the government had removed rent controls, and the weakening of the military dictatorship, which gave low-income households more hope that the settlements they rapidly built would not be bulldozed – see Cuenya, Armus, di Loreto et al 1990 and Cuenya, Almada, Armus et al 1990.

There are also the costs faced by particular low-income groups as they get 'legal' housing. For instance, the 20,000 households in Mumbai who were resettled from land beside the railway tracks to better quality and more secure accommodation had to learn how to manage the payment of regular utility bills (Patel, d'Cruz and Burra 2002). Interviews with the occupants of Santa Maria, an informal settlement in Greater Buenos Aires formed by a land invasion, reported that the cost of services took a high proportion of their household income. These households also had to make regular payments towards the cost of the land (their illegal occupation had been legalized, but the condition for doing so was that they had to pay towards the cost of the land and the public works) – and the cost of services, especially those that had been privatized, had risen to the point where this jeopardized their ability to keep up the payments of fixed instalments under the land tenure regularization scheme (Herzer, Di Virgilio, Lanzetta et al 2000).

(d) *Access to water* – and, in some instances, to sanitation and garbage collection. In many urban settings, particular low-income groups are paying particularly high prices for certain necessities – especially water. For instance, a review of data on what urban households pay for water per litre found that this varied by a factor of more than 1,000 – see Table 3.

Table 3: Differentials in the prices paid for water

	Price paid per litre (US dollars)	Price of 150 litres per day (US$)
Water tariff in Cairo	0.00004	0.006
Cooperative in Santa Cruz	0.00025-0.00055	0.04-0.08
Public tap in Bandung	0.00026	0.04
Utility in Lima	0.00028	0.042
Independent water provider in Asuncion	0.00035	0.05
House connection in Bandung	0.00038	0.06
Price of water from a standpipe in Ouagadougou	0.00048	.072
Water tariff in Amman	0.00061	0.09
Water vendor in Dhaka (1995)	0.00084	0.13
Price paid for water to standpipe operators in Nairobi	0.001-0.025	0.15-0.38
Average paid by urban households in East Africa with piped water connection (1997)	0.001	0.15
Water tariff in Ramallah	0.00111	0.17
Water from water point in Huruma (Nairobi)	0.0013	0.195
Kiosks in Kampala	0.0015-0.007	0.23-1.1
Standpipes in Dar es Salaam drawing water from mains	0.0015	0.23
Average paid by urban households in East Africa that lack piped water	0.002	0.3
Average price paid to vendors by low-income groups living in salinated areas in Jakarta (1991)	0.002	0.3
Water trucker in Lima	0.0024	0.36
Handcarts delivering to homes in Dar es Salaam	0.0035-0.0075	0.53-1.13
Water vendor in Bandung (1995)	0.0036	0.54
Price of water from tankers in Luanda in 1998	0.004-0.02	0.6-3.0
Price of water from a handcart in Conakry	0.004	0.6
Average price paid to vendors in East African urban areas (1997)	0.0045	0.7
Bicycle water vendor in Kampala, delivering to non-serviced area	0.0054-0.0108	0.81-1.6
Water from public tap in Lae (Papua New Guinea)	0.00596	0.9
Water from vendor in Kibera (Nairobi)	0.0065	0.97
Those purchasing 55-gallon barrels of water from vendors in Tegucigalpa (US$1.75 per barrel)	0.0072	1.08
Vendor in Male (1995)	0.011	1.7
Vendor in Kibera (Nairobi) during local water shortages	0.013	1.95
Water from a tanker in Luanda for those in areas distant from water sources	0.02	3.0

SOURCES: Cairo, Amman and Ramallah - Saghir, Schiffler and Woldu 2000; Santa Cruz, Lima ,Tegucigalpa and Asuncion - Solo 2000; Bandung, Male, Dhaka and Lae - McIntosh and Yñiguez 1997; Ouagadougou and Conakry: - Water and Sanitation Program 2000; Nairobi- Champetier and Farid 2000; East Africa - Thompson, Porras, Wood et al 2000; Huruma (Nairobi) - Pamoja Trust 2001; Kampala - Champetier and Wandera 2000;

Jakarta - McGranahan, Jacobi, Songsore et al 2001; Dar es Salaam – Champetier, Sykes and Wandera 2000; Luanda - Cain, Daly and Robson 2002; Kibera (Nairobi) - Katui-Katua and McGranahan 2002.

Households who rent rooms or who live in illegal settlements may be paying particularly high prices for water (see, for instance, Rakodi and Withers 1995 for Harare, and SPARC 1985 for pavement dwellers in Mumbai). Table 3 shows the very large variations in water prices, both between cities and between different sources in the same city. Those who rely on water vendors or water kiosks (generally those living in illegal settlements) generally pay much more per litre than those who have piped water connections. For instance, in a study covering urban areas in Kenya, Uganda and Tanzania in 1997, the average price paid for water per litre by households with piped water connections was less than one quarter the average price paid by those with no household connections to water vendors (Thompson, Porras, Wood et al 2000). Those living in settlements with no piped provision generally pay most: for instance water from water kiosks in Kampala was generally much cheaper than water from bicycle vendors who delivered to non-serviced areas (Champetier and Wandera 2000). Those living in peripheral locations generally pay the most; the prices of water from tankers in Luanda varied considerably, depending on the settlement's distance from water sources (Cain, Daly and Robson 2002).

For many low-income urban households, the payments made to water vendors represent a major item of household expenditure – often 10 percent and sometimes 20 percent of household income – with particular case studies showing even higher proportions.[61] Many urban households also have to pay for garbage collection and for access to latrines. There is a growing literature showing the extent to which large sections of the population in many cities have no sanitation facility at all in their home – and public or communal provision is so poor or so expensive that they resort to defecation outside, or what is termed in the Philippines as 'wrap and throw'.[62] Where pay-to-use public toilets have developed, these can take up a significant proportion of poor households' incomes. For instance, in Kumasi, the cost of using a pay-toilet for a family of five, each using it only once a day, would be equivalent to at least 10 percent of a basic wage (Devas and Korboe 2000).

There is also the issue of water utilities charging rising block tariffs for water, which is meant to benefit poorer households (low-volume users) through a cross-subsidy, with funds drawn from charging more to high-volume users (presumed to be the higher-income groups). But, in many instances, poorer households only have shared water connections, and this means that the water for these shared connections is charged at higher rates (see Devas and Korboe 2000 for a discussion of this in relation to Kumasi).

(e) *Health care*. Various studies show that the costs of health care and medicines represent a significant share of household expenditures or urban poor household expenditures. A socio-economic survey in Kampala in 1990 highlighted the high proportion of total household income spent on education and health care (Bigsten and Kayizzi-Mugerwa 1992). Ghosh, Ahmad and Maitra 1994 found that 10 percent or more of the income of 'slum' households in two of the four cities they looked at went on health care. Dinye 1995 noted that 15 percent of household expenditure among a sample of households in a low-income settlement in Kumasi was going on health. A study of poverty in Honduras found that 9 percent of expenditures in urban areas were going on health care (World Bank 2001b).

But there are also the costs related to the inadequacies in health care that do not appear in expenditure surveys. For instance, a study in a 'slum' area in Khulna, Bangladesh, highlighted the very large economic burden caused by poor health associated with poor quality housing and lack of basic services – and how the economic cost in terms of income lost from days off work and from medical expenses was greater than the cost of improving the infrastructure to eliminate the health problems (Pryer 1993). A comparable study in Dhaka showed that ill-health was the most important cause of deterioration in financial status among Dhaka slum households (Pryer 2003). In Karachi, the low-cost sanitation system

---

[61] See, for instance, Cairncross 1990; see also Devas and Korboe 2000, Ghosh, Ahmad and Maitra 1994, Aegisson 2001, Moser 1996 and Etemadi 2000 for other examples of low-income households paying high costs or high proportions of their income on water and/or sanitation.
[62] This literature is reviewed in Hardoy, Mitlin and Satterthwaite 2001; see also Burra, Patel and Kerr 2003 and UN–Habitat 2003a.

supported by the Orangi Pilot Project brought the cost of good quality sewers down to the point where the cost of installation per household is likely to be less than the savings made in one year from reduced time off work and treatment costs, because of improved health (Orangi Pilot Project 1995). In settlements where there are high risks of malaria, low-income households can spend a significant proportion of their income on mosquito coils or sprays (see, for instance, Thomas, Seager, Viljoen et al 1999). As noted earlier, expenditure on health care by low-income groups is often not an indicator of the income they need for health care, as they cannot afford to seek treatment or purchase the most appropriate medicines. Devas and Korboe 2000 noted that, with the introduction of charges for health care in Ghana, many people in Kumasi no longer used the health care services when sick or injured, or they sought cheaper alternatives.

(f) *Energy* (including fuel for cooking and heating water and, where needed, space heating and electricity). Households with below poverty line incomes in Dhaka had 7.7 percent of their expenditures going on fuel in 1995, but the poorest groups within 'the poor' had 10 percent of expenditures going on fuel (Islam, Huda, Narayan et al 1997). Other studies showing that the costs of energy are a significant proportion of expenditures for low-income groups include Mozambique, Government of et al, 1998, Grootaert 1996 and Ghosh, Ahmad and Maitra 1994. Where low-income households obtain electricity through shared electricity meters, this can result in them being charged higher rates because of rising block tariffs.[63]

(g) *Child care.* This can be costly for low-income households where all adult members have to find income-earning opportunities, but there may be no low-cost or no-cost solutions – although, often, this difficulty is solved through reciprocity at community level or by leaving older siblings in charge. It is also a difficulty often 'solved' by leaving young children unattended at home or by leaving siblings in charge of the very young, with all the attendant risks this brings.

It is also likely that many low-income urban households have other costs that go unrecognized by those who set poverty lines, including payments to community-based organizations and the payment of fines (for instance, for illegal street-vending). The cost of funerals can be particularly onerous in areas where there is high child mortality or high adult mortality (for instance, in areas where the incidence of AIDS is particularly high). Various studies have also shown how many urban poor groups are paying a significant proportion of their income on debt repayments (see, for instance, CARE/Bangladesh 1998, Amis and Kumar 2000, Kwon 1998). Many urban households also have to face the cost of eviction – where they are forcibly evicted from a settlement and lose many household possessions. Many of those who are evicted also lose the investments they made in building and improving their homes. There are also other costs, such as the disruption to livelihoods and to social networks that often have great importance in avoiding deprivation.[64]

Finally, the way that poverty lines are defined usually does not make any allowance for households to save, as all resources would be required to satisfy basic needs (Mejía and Vos 1997). But, as is increasingly recognized, savings can have particular importance for low-income urban households because of the emergency credit that community-based savings groups can provide to help cope with shocks and stresses.[65] As will be discussed in more detail later, community-based savings schemes are also often the basis on which schemes to support community members acquire and develop their own homes are developed.

---

[63] See Devas and Korboe 2000 for an example in Kumasi and Patel, d'Cruz and Burra 2002 for an example in Mumbai.

[64] There is a very considerable literature now on the cost of evictions for low-income households and the extent to which this creates poverty – see, for instance, the publications of the Asian Coalition for Housing Rights over the last 15 years (including the most recent – Asian Coalition for Housing Rights 2003); also the publications of the Centre on Housing Rights and Evictions (COHRE) and the papers in Vol 6, No 1 of *Environment and Urbanization* 1994, which was on evictions, especially Murphy and Anana 1994 and COHRE 1994.

[65] Many urban poor federations have at their base community or group savings schemes from which members can draw funding to cope with emergencies – see, for instance, Patel and d'Cruz 1993, Boonyabancha 2003 and Patel and Mitlin 2004.

b. The variations in what poor urban households spend on different non-food items

Clearly, low-income households cannot be spending high proportions of their incomes on all the above items (i.e. spending 15–30 percent of their income on housing, 10 percent on fuel, 10–20 percent on water and toilets, 10–15 percent on transport, 5–10 percent on health care and 5–10 percent on keeping children at school…..) because this would leave little or no money for food. Data on 'average non-food expenditures' among urban populations or for particular groups (for instance, the poorest 20 percent) are easily mis-interpreted if there is no recognition of the variation between low-income households in any city with regard to which of the items noted above are the main non-food expenditures.

To keep total expenditures on housing, infrastructure and services to what they can afford, each individual or household makes choices about the trade-offs that best suit them with regard to location for access to income-earning opportunities, housing size and quality, degree of security of tenure, and quality of infrastructure and service provision. Most low-income groups in urban areas will prioritize location in relation to income-earning opportunities above housing quality because without income, they cannot survive. For instance, young single people will often rent space in very overcrowded central tenements or boarding houses because these provide easy access to places where income can be earned (for instance, within casual labour markets or jobs with very long hours) and because this keeps down accommodation costs. Cheap boarding houses may be particularly useful for individuals who come to cities for short periods (for instance, circular or temporary migrants). Housing costs may be minimized and central locations ensured by sleeping in public places, parks, graveyards or streets. In Bombay/Mumbai, one of the key reasons why so many people live in tiny shacks constructed on pavements is that this allows them to walk to the places where they earn their income (ibid, SPARC 1985). The many poor households in Mumbai that live or used to live in tiny shacks next to railway tracks also did so because of the good location this provided for income-earning opportunities (Patel, d'Cruz and Burra 2002). In most cities, there are central districts with high levels of overcrowding (for instance, in tenements or cheap boarding houses), which arise because their inhabitants have incomes that are too low to allow them to afford the transport costs if they lived further away in less overcrowded dwellings (Hardoy and Satterthwaite 1989).

Other low-income groups will prioritize more space – for instance, low-income households with children will be more likely to seek more room, but to find this they generally need to live in less central locations – for instance, as they build their own home or purchase one in a less central informal or illegal settlement. Here, they may also have good possibilities of (eventually) getting legal tenure of the land they occupy and so become owner-occupiers which, in turn, means that their house becomes a valuable capital asset. But for low-income households to find such land usually means a peripheral location, with high costs for transport to and from work and services. The priority an individual or household gives to access to infrastructure and services often increases when they have or plan to have children. Analyses of the different housing sub-markets used by low-income groups in any city show these different trade-offs and how they are realized within the possibilities and constraints of each city (Hardoy and Satterthwaite 1989, *Environment and Urbanization* 1989). Obviously, the choices made by each individual or household with regard to their preferred trade-offs between these different housing sub-markets are influenced by age, sex, household composition, source of income, plans…… These choices are much influenced by (among other things) the nature of the city economy, the distribution of income, the land market (and land-owning structure), the measures taken by governments to help or hinder people and companies acquiring and developing land for housing, the quality and efficiency of companies and utilities responsible for provision for water, sanitation, drainage, schools, public transport……………

Thus, to be an accurate reflection of the income needed to avoid poverty, a poverty line needs to be set within each local context, or adjusted to each local context. It has to be set at an income that allows the individual or household to not only have an adequate diet but also to afford safe accommodation with adequate basic infrastructure and services (water, sanitation, drainage, garbage removal, fuel, health care ……), as well as the costs of transport (for instance, to and from work and essential services), clothing and, for households with children, keeping children at school. As a recent report on urban demography noted, without knowledge of the full range of circumstances in each neighbourhood or district, it is difficult to specify the level of income required to avoid poverty (Montgomery, Stren, Cohen and Reed 2003). A lack of local data means that governments establish simple, administratively feasible poverty lines, and the key question is how many families get mis-classified (ibid); the evidence in this section suggests that a significant proportion of urban dwellers do get mis-classified.

V. THE POTENTIAL OPPORTUNITIES OF PROVIDING 'HIDDEN' INCOME OR CONSUMPTION IN URBAN AREAS

The discussion above suggests that most urban households need substantially higher cash incomes to avoid poverty than most rural households, especially if they live in the larger and/or more prosperous cities. But in most or all nations, a proportion of low-income urban households will enjoy better quality infrastructure and basic services than most low-income rural households, and this can be considered an important 'hidden additional income' (or perhaps, more correctly, hidden consumption) that is associated with urban areas. These include goods and services that are not delivered through the market (including public goods).

These may arise because:
- infrastructure and services are provided by governments or local institutions (for instance, NGOs or charities) free or below their actual cost;
- goods may be available with prices that are lowered through subsidies (for instance, as government subsidies lower the price of certain staple foods or fuels);
- services or credit are available at prices that are lowered through subsidies (for instance, for some public transport systems or for housing finance); or
- there is a wider range of public goods and of goods and services provided by private enterprises, with lower prices and better quality due to economies of scale and proximity for the institutions or enterprises providing them.

Poverty lines do not capture most of these. If poverty is measured only by consumption expenditure, a household living in a home for which they have secure tenure and provision for piped water, connection to a sewer and their solid waste collected, will appear just as poor as a household with none of these if they have the same expenditure level. The same is true for access to 'public' services provided free or at below cost, especially schools, health centres, solid waste removal and emergency services. At one extreme, in well-governed urban centres where the potential economies of scale, agglomeration and proximity are used in the provision of infrastructure and services, most households with incomes that are close to the poverty line may not 'live in poverty'. They can send their children to school and use health care services because these are free or efficiently provided, so costs are kept down. They can live in legal housing where they are not in constant fear of eviction, and where their housing is served with regular, safe, piped water supplies and with adequate provision for sanitation, drainage and garbage removal. At the other extreme, in urban centres with very poor or inadequate 'governance', households with incomes that are close to the poverty line may have none of these. Indeed, many households with incomes significantly above the poverty line may 'live in poverty' because provision for infrastructure and services is so inadequate.

Datt and Jolliffe 1999 note that, in Egypt, the measurement of poverty fails to incorporate some important aspects of individual welfare, including the consumption of public goods such as schools, health services and public sewage facilities. Khusro 1999 notes the difficulty of calculating expenditure on public goods – as people typically do not 'purchase' their literacy, education and health goods in the same manner that they purchase food and other necessities. In India, these are either heavily subsidized or supplied at the state's expense, and personal expenditure data do not capture the (often very large) consumption met from government services. Thus, a focus on measuring and monitoring poverty using poverty lines can greatly understate the potential to reduce poverty through public goods (including those provided by non-government organizations).

It is likely that there are substantial benefits for large sections of the urban population from cheaper or more readily available or better quality infrastructure, services and goods (both public and private) – but:
- it is not certain that all or even most of the urban poor benefit; and

- it is difficult to separate out benefits that arise from 'urban bias', in the sense of government investment, expenditure or other measures benefiting urban dwellers more than rural dwellers, from benefits that arise in urban areas because of the more concentrated demand and economies of scale and proximity for the supply of infrastructure and services.

Certainly, public agencies responsible for the provision of piped water and sewers to people's homes in urban areas often fail to cover their costs through connection fees and user charges, and this means that those who receive connections are receiving subsidies. But a large proportion of the urban population do not receive either piped water to their homes or connection to sewers. Indeed, most urban centres in sub-Saharan Africa and many in Asia have no sewers and little or no piped water network; for those urban centres that do, it is largely middle- and upper-income groups that are served (Hardoy, Mitlin and Satterthwaite 2001, UN Habitat 2003a). This is even the case in the 'large cities' where it might be assumed that 'urban biases' are most evident. Urban populations generally benefit more from publicly funded schools (as can be seen, for instance, by higher enrolment rates in schools for urban populations compared to rural populations in most nations) and (probably) hospitals and clinics but, again, there are large sections of the urban poor in most nations who are ill-served or not served at all; the example of low-income households having to pay for 'private schools' in Orangi in Karachi because they could not get into government schools was noted earlier. Primary school enrolment among the 'slum' populations of Dhaka and Chittagong is much lower than the national and rural averages (UNICEF 2000). The inhabitants of illegal settlements in cities often face difficulties in getting their children into schools or accessing other 'public goods' because this requires a legal address that they do not have. A few empirical studies in low-income areas of cities have shown how their inhabitants do not have access to the public goods and services that are available locally (see, for instance, Misra 1990). Khusro 1999 comments that it is really only the highest-income groups that 'purchase' education and health services through private schools and health care (and so their use of these is reflected in expenditure data) but, in many urban contexts, this is not correct, as poor households turn to private provision because there is no public provision or they are denied access to public provision. However, the lack of local data makes it difficult to estimate how widespread this is.

Thus, although the literature on 'urban bias' assumes that urban populations are better served by infrastructure and services than rural populations (see, for instance, World Bank 1990) because they are much closer to schools, hospitals, water mains and sewers, the extent to which this benefits poorer urban dwellers is not clear. Proximity does not imply access.

The other difficulty with regard to whether or not there is 'urban bias' is separating out urban advantages from urban biases. Most urban contexts provide economies of scale, proximity and density that cheapen the unit cost of providing good quality infrastructure and services (Hardoy, Mitlin and Satterthwaite 2001, Montgomery, Stren, Cohen and Reed 2003). Average incomes are also generally higher in urban areas than in rural areas, which also means more capacity to pay for these. The unit cost of providing piped water to each housing unit and a connection to a sewer or drainage network falls as density increases, while the cost per person of many elements of a water and sewer network (for instance, water storage and treatment, sewage treatment) comes down as settlement population increases. So the cost of removing deprivations associated with a lack of provision for piped water, sanitation and drainage is usually less per person in urban areas – and if incomes are higher, the gap between good quality provision and what can be paid for is also reduced. There are similar cost savings or economies of scale or proximity for public transport and many educational, health and emergency services, which makes it cheaper per household served to provide these in urban areas (or larger urban centres). However, rural contexts may allow less expensive forms of adequate sanitation from a health and convenience perspective than most urban households.[66]

Again, the community-managed sewer construction programme in Orangi in Karachi (which also set a model that has been implemented in other urban areas or districts of Pakistan) serves as an example, as the sewers were constructed with full cost-recovery from those who were connected. Clearly, in most

---

[66] The cheapest forms of 'improved' sanitation, such as ventilated improved pit latrines, become increasingly inappropriate at higher densities and with larger settlements.

rural contexts, the unit costs of constructing comparable sewers would have been much higher. Yet, the construction of these sewers in Orangi was not urban bias but good local use of demand and innovations to keep down unit costs. In Thailand, the Urban Community Development Office supported a great range of urban-based community organizations with low-interest loans from 1992 to 2000, and this led to improvements in housing conditions and in income – but with loans that fully recovered their costs, these could not be construed as 'urban bias'.[67] Where urban populations are served with better quality infrastructure and services than rural populations, for which they pay the full cost, this is not 'urban bias'. It might also be argued that where urban populations are served with better quality infrastructure and services that arise from funding drawn from urban tax bases, this is also not 'urban bias'.[68]

The proportion of urban dwellers who benefit from 'urban advantages', and the extent of this benefit, depends heavily on the quality of local governance. In well-governed cities, these potential advantages are realized, often with funding drawn only from the city's own tax/revenue base. Efficient public, private or community action can lower the income that a household requires to 'avoid poverty' or some aspects of poverty. A well-managed city or municipal system for piped water and provision for sanitation, drainage and garbage removal (generally more common in urban than in rural areas) can greatly reduce the cost of adequate quality accommodation with basic services. Or an upgrading programme to provide or improve water supplies, sanitation, drainage, paved roads and paths in existing low-income settlements can, in effect, move many inhabitants out of 'living in poverty', as their costs are not increased and the quality of their homes is greatly improved.[69] Effective public or non-profit private provision for schools, health care and child care can also lower the income needed by households to avoid poverty. An efficient public transport system can cut the costs of access to employment, while well-managed housing credit schemes can cut the cost of access to adequate housing – and to acquiring housing that then becomes an important asset (Mitlin 1997, Boonyabancha 2001). There are also many examples of relatively low-income urban households gaining access to land for housing at below market prices, through invasion or illegal occupation or purchasing illegal sub-divisions – although the capacity to acquire a land site for housing that is secure and below market price is now less common, as even the informal or illegal means of obtaining land for housing have become highly commercialized in many cities.

Thus, if efficient public, private or community action to improve housing and basic services is concentrated in urban areas, this would lower the 'poverty line income' needed for those urban households who benefited from such action. If this was provided at no subsidy or at subsidies that were no more than those used to subsidize goods, services or investments in rural areas, it would not be urban bias.

However, while urban populations can benefit from 'hidden income' or consumption where there is 'good governance', they can also suffer more where there is 'bad' or 'no' governance. The advantages of having larger and more concentrated populations for the provision of infrastructure and services turn into disadvantages with regard to environmental health risks, if there is no provision. This may help explain why, in many nations, infant and child mortality rates are not much lower in urban areas than in rural areas – as here, the potential urban advantage for cheaper and better quality infrastructure and services is not realized. As noted earlier, there are hundreds of millions of urban households who have no access to safe and sufficient water supplies, and no provision for sanitation and drainage. Many have inadequate or no access to schools and health care services, even if they have incomes that are above the poverty line.

---

[67] The Urban Community Development Office became the Community Organizations Development Institute in 2000, and supports both rural and urban community organizations (Boonyabancha 2003 and 2004).

[68] This may still be contentious, with the rural proponents arguing that cities' larger tax base is, in part, the result of terms of trade or government policies favouring urban areas, and the urban proponents arguing that it arises from the fact that cities concentrate a much higher proportion of economic activities than they do populations, and emphasizing how much city enterprises or populations contribute to national tax revenues.

[69] Costs may be increased, where cost-recovery is sought, but major improvements can often be made at low cost, with cost-recovery through community-managed schemes such as the sewers installed in Orangi, supported by the Orangi Pilot Project. Costs may also be reduced – for instance, where the inhabitants previously had to purchase water from water vendors, and the costs that households pay towards the upgrading costs are actually less per month than they previously paid to these vendors.

Many urban governments are, in effect, anti-poor (and help create poverty), through unnecessary rules and regulations (including harassment and penalties for many informal enterprises) and eviction and resettlement programmes.[70] Amis 1999 noted that, even if local governments have a limited capacity to reduce poverty, they have a much greater capacity to create or exacerbate it.

Thus, many low-income urban dwellers suffer from forms of deprivation that are generally associated with poverty, however, it is not their low incomes that are the cause but, rather, the incapacity of public, private or non-profit institutions to ensure provision,[71] and the capacity of government institutions to contribute to impoverishment. Here, it is important to recognize the extent to which many forms of deprivation faced by poor households (and often many non-poor households) are more the result of weak, ineffective, unrepresentative or corrupt governments than of their income levels. As such, many forms of deprivation associated with poverty can be addressed by more competent and effective public or private institutions – and, in many urban areas, with little or no subsidy. Thus, there is considerable scope in most urban centres for supporting improvements in housing and living conditions and in basic services among lower-income households at low per capita costs and with a considerable degree of cost-recovery. This also suggests the need for poverty measures to include assessments of the quality and extent of provision for public goods. Minujin 1999 argues that provision for basic needs should be measured directly because this is not captured in a money-metric index. Certainly, in many Latin American nations, it is more common to have assessments of 'unsatisfied basic needs' as part of the official statistics used by governments to measure and monitor poverty, and there is some indication that this is becoming more common in other nations (see, for instance, the review of Poverty Reduction Strategy Papers in Mitlin 2004).

VI. OTHER LIMITATIONS OF POVERTY LINES

Perhaps not surprisingly, there is a large literature on the inappropriateness or limitations of poverty lines – both generally and specifically for urban areas.[72] These raise issues other than the extent to which poverty lines are set too low in relation to the cost of needs for large sections of the urban population, and the issue of whether urban poor groups benefit from 'hidden consumption'. One set of concerns is the extent to which they divide the urban population into the 'poor' and the 'non-poor', with little idea of the diversity within 'the poor' and the 'nearly poor' with regard to their deprivations, vulnerabilities and needs. Table 4 is a reminder of the diversity that is likely to occur in any urban area with regard to the form of poverty; of course, any poverty analysis should seek a greater disaggregation than this in, for instance, employment base, gender, ethnic group, age etc.

---

[70] See references in note 64.

[71] One study in the Indian city of Aligarh found that there were serious deficiencies for the whole city in terms of infrastructure and service provision, and that a higher income level did not necessarily mean a large diminution in household-level environmental problems. For instance, for drainage provision and garbage collection, there was only a marginal improvement as a household's income level rose. This points to serious environmental problems at the household level that prevail in the whole city, irrespective of economic level or of the size and quality of the housing in the area. Open defecation (i.e. with households having no provision for sanitation) is not restricted to the areas where the population has below poverty line incomes; see Aziz, Singh and Siddiqi 1995.

[72] For those related to urban areas see, for instance, Moser 1993, 1996 and 1998, Chambers 1995, *Environment and Urbanization* 1995a and 1995b, Rakodi 1995, Wratten 1995, Satterthwaite 1997a, Mitlin and Satterthwaite 2004.

Table 4: Different degrees of poverty in urban areas

Aspects of poverty	Degrees of poverty			
	Destitution	Extreme poverty	Poverty	At risk
Income	Income below the cost of a minimum food basket	Income just above the cost of minimum food basket but far too low to allow other necessities to be met	Income below a realistic poverty line* but enough to allow significant expenditure on non-food essentials	Income just above a realistic poverty line*
Housing with access to infrastructure and services	Homeless or no-cost shelter or close to no-cost shelter	Very little to spend on housing – often renting a room in a tenement or illegal or informal settlement	More accommodation options – e.g. slightly more spacious, better quality rental housing or capacity to self-build a house if cheap or free land is available; extent and quality of affordable options much influenced by government land, infrastructure and services policies	
Assets	Typically none or very little (although community-based savings group may provide access to credit for emergencies)		Often some capacity to save, especially within well-managed savings and credit scheme	
Vulnerability	Extreme vulnerability to food price rises, loss of income or illness or injury; often also to discrimination and unfair practices (from employers, landlords, civil servants, politicians, the law.......)		Similar kinds of vulnerability to those faced by people facing destitution or extreme poverty, although usually less severe; often vulnerability to running up serious debt burdens	

* A realistic poverty line would be one that was calculated based on real prices and costs in each city and which took into account the cost of non-food essentials (safe, secure housing, transport, water, sanitation, health care, keeping children at school..........) as well as the cost of an adequate diet.

One set of concerns about poverty lines is that they may be manipulated and so are not based on data (although the earlier discussions of the multiple ways in which poverty lines can be adjusted and the extent to which they are consistently set at levels that under-estimate the income needed to avoid poverty is in part related to this). It includes a concern that they may not be adjusted for inflation since inflation can make them obsolete very quickly, especially where no provision is made to adjust them in relation to rising costs (or the adjustments that are made systematically adjust them below the real rise in costs); the failure to adequately adjust poverty lines or poverty-reducing measures for inflation can be one of the ways in which higher-income groups allow an erosion of total expenditures on poverty reduction (Kanbur and Squire 2001).

Another set of concerns is the lack of attention given to intra-household differentials. Poverty lines are set based on household data, yet intra-household differentials often exist in consumption, allocation, and in use of household income and control of assets. As argued by Moser 1993 and Wratten 1995, individual members of a household do not have equal command over resources, and those with low entitlement to consume resources or use income due, for example, to age, gender or social status may be hidden within relatively prosperous households. For some time, researchers have attempted to see how resources are allocated within households, and why it matters from a policy perspective. This is also an important issue in the discussion of 'household' expenditure (see, for instance, Haddad, Hoddinott and Alderman 1997).

There is also the issue of vulnerability raised in Table 4 above. Poverty lines can be criticized for ultimately being a static measure that gives little idea of the processes that cause or help people avoid poverty. Income levels or consumption levels indicate symptoms of poverty and offer little indication of underlying causes, including discrimination and exploitation. They give little indication of particular circumstances that need particular responses (for instance, the erosion of purchasing power for state pensions that has put many older people at risk in various Latin American nations). They do not capture poorer households' responses and how their capacity to cope can be enhanced. They also do not capture the vulnerability of individuals or households to falling below the poverty line, but only the proportion who at the time of the survey were below it. So, no distinction is drawn between chronic and transient poverty – yet, households facing a temporary fall in income generally need a very different policy response to those who have long had or always had below poverty line incomes (Kanbur and Squire 2001).

The literature on livelihoods and on the importance for low-income groups of asset bases for avoiding or better coping with poverty has tended to focus on rural areas, although there is a growing urban literature (see, for instance, Moser 1998 and Rakodi with Lloyd Jones 2002). It may be that large sections of the urban population are particularly vulnerable to falling incomes or loss of income because of changes in urban labour markets, including the contraction in the number of secure jobs (in part from government retrenchments) and the increasing use by employers of sub-contracting, a greater reliance on casual labour and a greater use of home workers (Wratten 1995, Latapi and de la Rocha 1995, UNCHS 1996). Most urban dwellers have fewer possibilities to fall back on self-production or foraging than most rural dwellers as a way of coping with loss of income or employment. Moser 1998 also notes that focusing only on income overlooks future implications of current choices. Households that take children out of school to work because they cannot meet their needs may, for example, be more 'income rich', but will be more vulnerable in the near future and the children will lose out on the education that is important for their future earning capacity. Household expenditure data can also miss various other measures households take to cope with impoverishment, which then means they appear to be better off – including households doubling up and household members taking on more onerous and dangerous work.[73]

Conventional poverty lines also do not place a price on 'time'. Some goods and services may be provided 'free' for the poor, but if queuing time in an urban clinic or at a public standpipe or toilet increases, there is, in effect, a rise in the price of these services and a trade-off (often in women's time). Some authors suggest having a time-use indicator factored into any discussion on household transport expenditure. Some studies show how many low-income groups have to walk long distances to keep down their transport expenditures – see, for instance, Huq, Zahurul and Uddin 1996 for various cities in Bangladesh, and Barter 1999 for central Bombay/Mumbai and Jakarta. So while such individuals may be paying very little for transport costs, they are 'paying' through long journey times and extra physical efforts,

Most high-income nations have moved away from setting absolute poverty lines to setting relative poverty lines (for instance, set at 40 or 50 percent of the mean income), in recognition that this provides a better indication of the income needed to avoid poverty in that particular society. Within the discussion of how to define and set poverty lines in low- and middle-income nations, there is little mention of this, although some studies of poverty have used relative poverty lines.[74] Perhaps this is because of the limitations of relative poverty lines in tracking how absolute poverty levels change and in providing international comparisons, both of which are of particular interest to international agencies.

---

[73] See Latapí and de la Rocha 1995 for examples of the many measures taken by low-income households in Guadalajara to avoid impoverishment, which may make them more vulnerable and may make them appear to be better off in household surveys.

[74] See, for instance, a study of changes in poverty in Nigeria, 1985-96 (Nigeria 1998) and an analysis of poverty in South Africa (Ministry of the Office of the President 1995).

VII. BROADENING THE UNDERSTANDING AND MEASUREMENT OF POVERTY

Even if poverty lines are set at levels that reflect the income that poor urban dwellers need for food and non-food items, and adjusted to reflect spatial differences in the costs of necessities, this would still give an incomplete picture of deprivation. Table 5 shows eight different aspects of poverty (or of the deprivations associated with poverty). If poverty is defined and measured based only on income or consumption, it may also bias poverty reduction measures towards those that increase incomes or consumption, obscuring the many poverty-reducing measures that can be taken by addressing the other aspects of poverty listed below.

Table 5: Different aspects of poverty

1. *Inadequate and often unstable income* (and thus inadequate consumption of necessities, including food and, often, safe and sufficient water; often, problems of indebtedness, with debt repayments significantly reducing income available for necessities) and/or incapacity to afford rising prices for necessities (food, water, rent, transport, access to toilets, school fees.....)

2. *Inadequate, unstable or risky asset base* (non-material and material including educational attainment and housing) for individuals, households or communities, including those assets that help low-income groups cope with fluctuating prices or incomes.

3. *Poor quality and often insecure, hazardous and overcrowded housing.*

4. *Inadequate provision of 'public' infrastructure* (piped water, sanitation, drainage, roads, footpaths, etc.), which increases the health burden and often the work burden.

5. *Inadequate provision of basic services* such as day care/schools/vocational training, health care, emergency services, public transport, communications, law enforcement.

6. *Limited or no safety net* to ensure basic consumption can be maintained when income falls; also to ensure access to housing, health care and other necessities when these can no longer be paid for.

7. *Inadequate protection of poorer groups' rights through the operation of the law*: including laws, regulations and procedures regarding civil and political rights, occupational health and safety, pollution control, environmental health, protection from violence and other crimes, protection from discrimination and exploitation.

8. *Poorer groups' voicelessness and powerlessness within political systems and bureaucratic structures*, leading to little or no possibility of receiving entitlements to goods and services; of organizing, making demands and getting a fair response; and of receiving support for developing their own initiatives. Also, no means of ensuring accountability from aid agencies, NGOs, public agencies and private utilities, and of being able to participate in the definition and implementation of their urban poverty programmes.

NB. This table has been developed and modified since it was first drafted in 1995 for the Editorial of the October 1995 issue of *Environment and Urbanization*, and earlier versions of it have been published in various papers (for instance, Satterthwaite 1997a and 2001 and Mitlin and Satterthwaite 2004). It has drawn on many other people's work, especially Moser, Herbert and Makonnen 1993, Amis 1995, Chambers 1995, Wratten 1995, Baulch 1996, Moser 1996 and 1998.

Broadening the definition of poverty also helps to highlight the many factors that cause or contribute to poverty – see Figure 1.

Figure 1: Deprivations associated with urban poverty and their immediate external causes

	Incompetent or ineffective government limiting land supplies (e.g. inappropriate land use controls)	Homes built on illegal and often dangerous sites; better quality housing and serviced lots too expensive	No credit available to low-income groups to support land purchase and house building or improvement	
No organization providing survival income if income source is lost or falls; no insurance for assets (lost to disaster) or to cover health care costs	**Limited or no safety net**	**Poor quality and often insecure, hazardous and overcrowded housing**	**Inadequate provision for infrastructure and services (including water and sanitation) causing very large health burden**	Households living in illegal settlements where utilities or service providers refuse to operate
Debt repayments reducing available income				Service providers unaccountable and/or uninfluenced by democratic pressures
Dangerous jobs undertaken because of higher incomes – high risks of injury, illness and premature death	**Inadequate income**	POVERTY IN URBAN AREAS	**Poorer groups' voicelessness and powerlessness within political systems and bureaucratic structures**	Inefficiency or incapacity of utilities or service providers increasing gap between what is provided and what low-income households can afford
Income lost to illness and injury (and health care and medicine costs)				
Economy producing little opportunity for better incomes				Incompetent, ineffective or anti-poor police force
Health risks from under-nutrition and use of cheaper (poor quality) foods, fuels and water	**High prices paid for many necessities**	**Inadequate, unstable or risky asset base**	**Inadequate protection of poorer groups' rights through the operation of the law (including protection from discrimination)**	High levels of violence and other crimes
High/rising prices for necessities (food, water, rent, transport, school fees, pay-toilets.....)				Absence of rule of law and of support for poor realizing their civil and political rights and entitlements
	Short-term survival limiting asset building (e.g. capacity to save, children taken out of school to earn/collect water)	Asset base constantly eroded as it copes with illnesses, injuries and other stresses/shocks; limits of community reciprocity for low-income groups	No collateral for accessing credit to allow house or plot purchase or pay regularization costs or connection charges	Discrimination faced by particular groups with regard to access to income, housing, credit, services.... on basis of gender, age, nationality, class/ caste, ethnic group...

It may be difficult for those who are used to equating poverty with consumption-based criteria to accept this broader view of urban poverty, and it is difficult to incorporate many of the above aspects into quantitative measurements of poverty. But there are many examples of government, NGO or community-driven programmes that show it is important[75] because of the following:

---

[75] The rest of this section draws on many case studies showing the possibilities of reducing urban poverty by addressing these other aspects – see, for instance, Boonyabancha 2003 and 2004, Bolnick 1993, 1996, Schusterman and Hardoy 1997, Schusterman, Almansi, Hardoy et al 2001, most of the papers in *Environment and Urbanization* Vol 13, No 2, 2001, Hasan 1997, Porio and others 2004, Connolly 2004, Stein 2001, Alimuddin, Hasan and Sadiq 2004, Cavalcanti, Marquez and Costa 2004, Baumann, Bolnick and Mitlin 2004, Patel and Mitlin 2004, Weru 2004, Mitlin and Muller 2004, CODI 2004 and Cain, Daly and Robson 2002; also Satterthwaite 2002b and Mitlin and Satterthwaite 2004.

It helps shifts official perceptions of 'poor people' from being seen as 'consumers' or 'objects' of government policy to being seen as citizens with rights and legitimate demands who also have resources and capabilities that can contribute much to more effective poverty reduction programmes. It also implies a greater engagement with the groups facing deprivation.

It provides more entry points for poverty reduction and makes explicit the contributions that a much wider group of governmental, private sector, non-governmental and community-based organizations can make to poverty reduction, including many within each urban centre or urban district. This includes integrating measures to improve housing conditions and associated infrastructure and services into poverty reduction, and understanding the multiple linkages between these and addressing other aspects of poverty.

It highlights the importance of aspects other than income. Many case studies show how the deprivations associated with low income were much reduced without increasing incomes, through increasing assets or safety nets or improving housing conditions and basic services, or through political changes that allowed low-income groups to negotiate more support (or less harassment). Governments and NGOs generally have relatively little scope to directly increase poorer groups' incomes, but have much more scope to address the other aspects of poverty – for instance, improving or extending provision for basic services, removing constraints to finding or building better quality accommodation (and the land this needs), reducing police harassment of street vendors...........Some recent experiences with micro-finance and with AGETIP-type funds to support public works and employment may mean a greater than previously thought scope for addressing inadequate incomes. But within local, regional or national contexts where there is little scope for economic expansion (or for creating the conditions where this happens), more attention needs to be paid to the other aspects of poverty.

It recognizes the multiple roles that housing and neighbourhoods can have in urban poverty – and in poverty reduction. Housing in urban contexts generally has more influence on the incomes, asset bases, livelihoods, vulnerability and quality of life (and health) of low-income groups than external poverty reduction specialists recognize. It not only provides accommodation but is also:
- a location for getting to and from income-earning sources or possibilities and services;
- often a significant cost in individual or household budgets (so reducing this cost can mean more income available that can be spent on other necessities);
- for many, an important source of income (as a location where income-earning activities take place or where income is raised by renting out space);
- the primary defence against most environmental health risks (which are more serious in urban contexts than in rural contexts if there is no provision for water, sanitation and drainage, because of the larger and denser concentration of people and their wastes). As discussed earlier, for the hundreds of millions of urban dwellers living in poor quality accommodation, the health burdens they face from diseases and injuries contracted in the home and neighbourhood are a very large part of their total health burdens, and much greater than the burdens faced by those in good quality accommodation;
- a valuable asset, for those low-income households who are 'owner-occupiers' (even if this is in an illegal sub-division or squatter settlement where this ownership is not officially recognized);
- (for many low-income groups) the place where social networks are built that have great importance for households in helping them avoid poverty or cope with shocks and stresses.

Safer and more secure housing also provides households with more protection against the loss of their household assets from theft, accidental fires, extreme weather and disasters such as floods, landslides or earthquakes; it is almost always the poorer groups in urban areas that bear most of the costs from disasters (Hardoy, Mitlin and Satterthwaite 2001).

One important aspect of poverty for large sections of the urban population with low incomes is the insecurity of their accommodation, either because they are tenants (and have little legal protection from instant eviction or from other unfair practices by landlords) or because they live in illegal settlements (with little if any security or protection against bulldozing). It is interesting to note how much the organizations and federations formed by the urban poor or homeless in many different nations prioritize better quality or more secure housing. This is not because they would not prioritize increased incomes, but because this usually represents the best response to their poverty that is possible locally.

It may be assumed that higher incomes are the best way to help low-income households buy, build or rent better quality, safer, more secure housing. But there are often more possibilities for achieving this by making housing cheaper – for instance, through addressing the many constraints that unnecessarily increase the cost and reduce the supply of housing and of inputs into housing (land, materials, credit, infrastructure….). There are often many untapped resources that can help low-income households get better quality accommodation without increasing their incomes - especially through providing them with access to unused or under-utilized land on which they can organize the construction of housing. The key point is that good local governance, including support for urban poor organizations, can considerably reduce poverty, even if the urban poor's incomes are not increasing.

There can be powerful complementarities between different actions to reduce poverty – for instance, as improved basic service provision improves health, reduces fatigue (for instance, water piped into the home replacing a long trek to fetch and carry water from a standpipe) and increases real income (for instance, from less time off work from being ill or injured and lower medical costs).

Acting on the other aspects of poverty often increases incomes for poorer groups. Better quality housing and basic infrastructure and services can increase poor households' incomes. This may seem counter-intuitive, but better housing, infrastructure and services can increase real incomes through:

- enhancing income-earning opportunities for home enterprises (the scope and scale of which is often much improved by more space, electricity and better water supply and sanitation);
- expanded housing, allowing one or more room to be rented out;
- a good quality piped water supply that not only greatly improves the quality and quantity of water available to the household but, in many low-income settlements, also reduces the daily or weekly bill for water (which, for low-income households, often translates directly into increased food intake); and
- greatly reducing the loss of income from income earners having to take time off because they are sick or injured or because they are nursing other sick family members or because of the costs of medicines and treatment.

The importance of local resources and space for urban poor groups' own initiatives. Many of the more successful poverty reduction programmes have been achieved through urban poor groups successfully negotiating resources and/or room for autonomous action and/or a halt to previous harassment from local authorities – often with little or no foreign funding involved.[76] Also, often without much funding required from local authorities. If this is generally true, this greatly widens the scope of local actions that can help reduce poverty.

Where the poor's capacity to pay for improved services and for safer housing is limited, their capacity to negotiate with local authorities for less harassment (e.g. remove the threat of eviction for an illegal settlement) and very modest resources (e.g. the loan of equipment to help dig or clear drainage ditches, a weekly collection of solid waste....) can bring considerable benefits at very low cost.

The need for long-term support from governments and international agencies for 'good' local governance in urban centres. In many urban centres, provision for urban infrastructure and services is so limited and the capacity to expand it so weak that many of those with 'above poverty line' incomes, including even middle-income groups, cannot find housing with adequate provision for water and sanitation and for protection against natural disasters. 'Good' local governance has importance not only for what it can contribute to poverty reduction but also for what it stops local governments from doing that increases poverty (for instance, programmes to bulldoze informal settlements and 'resettlement' programmes that cause, exacerbate or deepen poverty).

---

[76] This is the case for most of the case studies noted in the previous footnote.

The need for local processes to influence priorities for poverty reduction in which the urban poor have influence. **As in many aspects of development policy, there needs to be a shift among specialists from recommending what should be done to recommending what local processes should be supported to influence what is done.**[77] It is difficult to generalize about what should receive priority because this depends on local circumstances and possibilities and on whose needs are being considered; it is easier to generalize about changes needed to local processes that allow local choices (in which urban poor groups have influence), mobilize local resources and remove local blockages. One cannot generalize about which of the eight different aspects of poverty noted above should receive priority. It depends so much on local circumstances and local capacities. It has to be guided by what is possible. Obviously, all households with low or unstable incomes want higher and more stable incomes – but there may be little scope for boosting these households' incomes, while there is considerable local capacity to work with urban poor groups to extend basic services, support improvements to housing and, for those in illegal settlements, provide more secure tenure. But the problem of what to prioritize is lessened if local authorities and other agencies involve urban poor groups in discussions of what to prioritize and why. Most successful poverty reduction initiatives strive to ensure that urban poor groups themselves have more influence on what is done and how it is done, and this often ends up in actions or programmes that address more than one aspect of poverty at the same time.

The above does not invalidate the utility of a poverty line but it suggests the need to be clear about what is omitted if poverty is only measured by consumption-based poverty lines, including public goods without a market (e.g. law and order, civil and political rights, negative externalities such as pollution) and those goods and services whose quality and extent of provision depend much on good governance.

VIII. WHAT THIS IMPLIES FOR THE MEASUREMENT OF POVERTY

The implications of what this paper has discussed with regard to the definition of poverty lines should be self-evident:

- *Greater attention to ensuring that poverty lines reflect the actual income that households need to avoid poverty (and to pay for the goods and services that they require to do so).* This means evaluating the validity of the measures currently used to define non-food needs or to calculate what allowance should be made for non-food needs in poverty lines. This also requires more attention to adjusting poverty lines by location so that they take into account the variations in the income needed to avoid poverty and do not under-state the scale of poverty in high-cost locations. This means a recognition of how much the income needed to avoid poverty is likely to vary between urban centres, so a single 'urban' and 'rural' adjustment will be inadequate.
- *Particular attention paid to incorporating more consideration of housing conditions and tenure, including the quality and extent of provision for water and sanitation or the income needed to get better quality housing into poverty measures;*[78] there needs to be more correspondence between figures on 'who is poor' and who is living in poverty (also noting that the quality of local governance will influence the extent of the association between income levels and housing and living conditions).

---

[77] This also raises issues of responsibility and accountability for researchers and staff from official agencies who make judgements about 'who is poor', as their judgments can influence who benefits and who does not from (say) infrastructure and services or safety nets. This is why our work has long emphasized the need for local judgements and decisions that are accountable to local populations, and subject to their influences.

[78] Both Mark Montgomery and James Garrett, when reviewing an earlier draft of this paper, pointed to the need for more attention to determining non-food needs and wondered why so little attention has been given to trying to measure the cost of non-food needs. This raises the issue of whether it would be more appropriate to set some standard for adequate housing (including secure tenure and adequate provision for water, sanitation and drainage) and investigate how much households would need to spend to get this standard. That is to do for key non-food needs what is often done for food needs (i.e. specify a standard and see how much it costs to reach that standard). This is certainly not easily done because definitions are also problematic (what is 'adequate' for housing, for water and sanitation and how this varies with context, what is 'secure' tenure) and data often deficient or lacking.

- *Recognition of the need to incorporate non-income aspects of poverty into official measures and monitoring*, including those with little correlation to income.
- *Avoidance of the US$ 1 or US$ 2 a day poverty line*, unless this can be demonstrated to have some local validity; these poverty lines are likely to be particularly inappropriate for higher-cost locations within nations.
- *The need to 'ground-truth' poverty statistics and poverty lines*. For instance, to look at housing conditions for households who have incomes close to the poverty line to see if their housing needs are met. This need for ground-truthing is particularly important for academics or institutions who want to compare poverty levels between nations or within nations between rural and urban areas, to avoid producing poverty statistics that bear no relation to local realities.
- While striving to make poverty measures more able to capture the scale and nature of deprivations that are linked to urban characteristics (and rural characteristics), also seek more integrated understandings of poverty, including the linkages between rural and urban dwellers and rural and urban economies, and the underlying causes of poverty that often contribute to both rural and urban poverty.

The implications for the measurement of poverty coming out of the discussions in Section VII are less certain. It is clear that there are many aspects of poverty that poverty lines do not measure – and cannot measure. Some may be addressed by household surveys and censuses that give more attention to housing and living conditions and to the quality and extent of infrastructure and service provision. If the discussion of how poverty is measured or should be measured is brought more into the public domain, especially within low- and middle-income nations, this should encourage innovations that make this more effective. As a recent review of urban demography noted:

"As China and other poor countries become more urban, the limitations of urban poverty estimates cannot be left to delicately worded footnotes and rueful caveats. Urbanization underscores the need for rigorous justification of the basis for urban poverty estimates and clear statements of the limits and uncertainties that surround such estimates" (Montgomery, Stren, Cohen and Reed 2003, page 184).

However, for most urban settings, perhaps a more pressing need is for attention to be paid to improving and expanding the local information base for the measurement of all aspects of poverty. This is to support local actions for poverty reduction and to support local processes in determining what should be done and how it should be done (including more space and scope for urban poor groups and their organizations and for local government). Household surveys that are based on representative samples for national populations (including the Demographic and Health Surveys and the Living Standards Measurements Surveys) are of little use to local actions because they do not identify who is suffering from deprivation and where they live. They may have sample sizes large enough to indicate conditions in 'urban areas' or even between size classes of cities (see Montgomery, Stren, Cohen and Reed 2003), but this is still no use to city and municipal authorities who need local detail. They need to know not only the proportion of people in their jurisdiction who lack provision (for instance, lacking water piped to their home) but also where they live. You cannot start a programme to extend provision for piped water if you do not know which households lack provision. Yet, there is surprisingly little consideration of the data needed to support local action or of the potential role of local authorities or other local bodies in contributing to a better understanding of poverty and more effective actions to reduce it. Most national governments and international agencies may have supported decentralization and local democracy but they have not supported the changes these require in official statistical services.

Four possible ways to address this:
- Ensuring that census data are available to local authorities and other local bodies in forms that allow their use in identifying and acting on deprivations (i.e. the availability of small-area data); it is not clear how many national governments ensure that local governments get census data in a form that is useful to them, but this appears to be rare (see Navarro 2001). Of course, there is the problem for many sub-Saharan African nations and some other low-income nations that censuses are rare and, for those that are held, often inaccurate.

- Complementing national household surveys with surveys of particular cities; see, for instance, the survey of Nairobi's informal settlements, which produced a wealth of information about health problems that was structured to fit within and complement the national demographic and health survey (APHRC 2002).

- Supporting local initiatives to generate the data needed for action, including those that urban poor organizations can undertake themselves. There are now many examples from many different nations and cities of city-wide 'slum' surveys, of very detailed 'slum' enumerations and of 'slum' mapping undertaken by urban poor organizations and local NGOs. These provide very strong information bases for housing improvement, regularizing tenure (and so making the inhabitants' housing more secure) and improving infrastructure and services – and high levels of accountability and participation are built into them.[79] Many of these initiatives have also been the catalysts for large-scale initiatives for poverty reduction, in which representative organizations of the urban poor and local authorities worked in partnership.

- Local organizations that make it their task to draw together all available data which, supplemented with consultation and discussion, provide a much stronger local information base; this may be done by the local government or by other local institutions.[80] City or municipal governments often have a range of information that could be used to support better policies and actions (see Navarro 2001, Velasquez 1998), but it is usually scattered among different departments. If there is a recognition among international agencies of the need for more civil society engagement in defining, measuring and monitoring poverty, and in discussions of how to address it, perhaps all cities need local 'urban resource centres'.[81] These are the kinds of local institutions that could help develop more valid and detailed poverty statistics rooted in local realities, working with urban poor groups.

There is also an obvious need to deepen and make more relevant the questions asked in household surveys and censuses with regard to the quality and security of housing, and quality and extent of provision for infrastructure and services. Knowing who has access to a piped water system does not mean much if there are no data on the quality and regularity of the supply in the pipe and the ease of access. It may be obvious that accessing piped water from a standpipe 100 metres from the home that is shared with 1000 other households is not the same as having a connection in the home but many statistics on water provision do not distinguish between these.[82]

One possible criticism of what is stated above is that it has an unrealistic or even a romantic view of what the 'urban poor' can do, and gives too much weight to insisting that they be fully involved in discussions about how best to define and measure poverty – and then how to reduce it. Any agency that has worked at grassroots level with poor groups knows that it is difficult to mesh the institutional concerns of their funders with more open, transparent and participatory ways of working. It is often not easy to work in participatory ways with urban poor groups – indeed, such groups are often full of complex conflicts which make any consensus on priorities difficult to achieve.[83] Many individuals and groups among the urban poor have a profound distrust of all external agencies, often rooted in their unsatisfactory previous experiences with such agencies.

---

[79] See, for instance, Patel, d'Cruz and Burra 2002, Weru 2004, Asian Coalition for Housing Rights 2004, Patel 2004, Orangi Pilot Project-Research and Training Institute 2002, Glockner, Mkanga and Ndezi 2004 and CODI 2004.

[80] See Navarro 2001 for an example of how this was done for two medium size Argentine towns; Velasquez 1998 for how this was done by urban observatories in different parts of the city of Manizales in Colombia. For examples of community-driven surveys, see Weru 2004 for how this is done in Nairobi; and Burra, Patel and Kerr 2003, Patel, d'Cruz and Burra 2002 and Patel 2004 for how these were used in resettlement programmes and community toilet programmes. See also Orangi Pilot Project - Research and Training Institute 2002 for an example of mapping for community-driven water and sanitation in Karachi, and Glockner, Mkanga and Ndezi 2004 for an example of such mapping in Dar es Salaam. The urban resource centres in Karachi and Cape Town are also examples of local institutions that help generate and disseminate the information needed to support locally driven processes in which urban poor groups have influence.

[81] See, for instance, the work programme of the Urban Resource Centre in Karachi (URC 1994, Hasan 1999).

[82] See UN Habitat 2003a.

[83] See Weru 2004.

But the recommendations made here are based on experiences that have been tried and tested in many different nations.[84] These also show that when one seeks to reconcile 'what is the most effective way to reduce urban poverty' with 'what is possible within a locality', one of the critical determinants of success is **the quality of the relationship between 'the poor' and the organizations or agencies** which have resources or powers that can help address one or more aspects of the deprivations they suffer.

Obviously, the extent of success also depends on:

- the extent to which such organizations or agencies have resources or decision-making powers that can support urban poor groups;
- the space given by such organizations to urban poor groups in defining priorities and developing responses;
- how urban poor groups are organized, and whose interests they represent; most of the examples of success are drawn from nations where organizations and federations of the urban poor have developed in ways that make them representative of and accountable to their members (and with women having key roles).

And obviously, the quality of this relationship between 'the poor' and all local or external agencies is influenced by these agencies' transparency and accountability to urban poor groups. But the experiences of the urban poor federations and of many other government or international initiatives who worked with urban poor groups shows how much poor groups and their community organizations can achieve with limited resources, where they have good relationships with local (and other) organizations and appropriate support for their actions. Those concerned with the definition and measurement of poverty need to consider how their work can support this.

---

[84] See, for instance, the references listed in footnote 75.

REFERENCES

Abrams, Charles (1964), *Man's Struggle for Shelter in an Urbanizing World*, MIT Press, Cambridge, USA.

Aegisson, Gunnar (2001*), Building Civil Society: Starting with the Basics*, One World Action, London, 32 pages.

Alder, Graham (1995), "Tackling poverty in Nairobi's informal settlements: developing an institutional strategy", *Environment and Urbanization*, Vol 7, No 2, October, pages 85-107.

Alimuddin, Salim, Arif Hasan and Asiya Sadiq (2004), "The work of the Anjuman Samaji Behbood in Faisalabad, Pakistan" in Diana Mitlin and David Satterthwaite (editors), *Empowering Squatter Citizen*, Earthscan Publications, London.

Amis, Philip (1995), "Making sense of urban poverty", *Environment and Urbanization*, Vol 7, No 1, April, pages 145-157.

Amis, Philip (1999), *Urban Economic Growth and Poverty Reduction*, Urban Governance, Partnerships and Poverty Research Working Paper 2, International Development Department, University of Birmingham, Birmingham, 45 pages.

Amis, Philip and Sashi Kumar (2000), "Urban economic growth, infrastructure and poverty in India: lessons from Visakhapatnam", *Environment and Urbanization*, Vol 12, No 1, April, pages 185-197.

Anzorena, Jorge, Joel Bolnick, Somsook Boonyabancha, Yves Cabannes, Ana Hardoy, Arif Hasan, Caren Levy, Diana Mitlin et al (1998), "Reducing urban poverty; some lessons from experience", *Environment and Urbanization*, Vol 10, No 1, April, pages 167-186.

APHRC (2002), *Population and Health Dynamics in Nairobi's Informal Settlements*, African Population and Health Research Center, Nairobi, 256 pages.

Appadurai, Arjun (2001), "Deep democracy: urban governmentality and the horizon of politics", *Environment and Urbanization*, Vol 13, No 2, October, pages 23-43.

Asian Coalition for Housing Rights (1989), "Evictions in Seoul, South Korea", *Environment and Urbanization*, Vol 1, No 1, April, pages 89-94.

Asian Coalition for Housing Rights (2001), "Building an urban poor people's movement in Phnom Penh, Cambodia", *Environment and Urbanization*, Vol 13, No 2, October, pages 61-72.

Asian Coalition for Housing Rights (2003), "How poor people deal with evictions", *Housing by People*, Number 15, October, Asian Coalition for Housing Rights, Bangkok, 48 pages.

Asian Coalition for Housing Rights (2004), "Negotiating the right to stay in the city", *Environment and Urbanization*, Vol 16, No 1, pages 9-26.

Asian Development Bank (2004), *Poverty Profile of the People's Republic of China*, Asian Development Bank, Manila.

Aziz, A, A L Singh and R H Siddiqi (1995), *Aligarh Environment Study*, Aligarh Muslim University, Aligarh, 72 pages.

Bapat, Meera and Indu Agarwal (2003), "Our needs, our priorities; women and men from the 'slums' in Mumbai and Pune talk about their needs for water and sanitation", *Environment and Urbanization*, Vol 15, No 2, October, pages 71-86.

Barbosa, Ronnie, Yves Cabannes and Lucia Moraes (1997), "Tenant today, *posseiro* tomorrow", *Environment and Urbanization*, Vol 9, No 2, October, pages 17-41.

Barter, Paul A (1999), "Transport and urban poverty in Asia. A brief introduction to the key issues", *Regional Development Dialogue*, Vol 20, No 1 (Spring), pages 143-163.

Baulch, B (1996), "The new poverty agenda: a disputed consensus" , *IDS Bulletin*, Vol 27, No 1, pages 1-10.

Baumann, Ted, Joel Bolnick and Diana Mitlin (2004), "The age of cities and organizations of the urban poor; the work of the South African Homeless People's Federation" in Diana Mitlin and David Satterthwaite (editors), *Empowering Squatter Citizen*, Earthscan Publications, London.

Beck, Tony (1994), *The Experience of Poverty: Fighting for Respect and Resource in Village India*, Intermediate Technology Publications, London, 221 pages.

Beijaard, Frans, "Rental and rent-free housing as coping mechanisms in La Paz, Bolivia", *Environment and Urbanization*, Vol 7, No 2, October, 1995, pages 167-182.

Bigsten, A and Steve Kayizzi-Mugerwa (1992), "Adoption and distress in the urban economy: a study of Kampala households", *World Development*, Vol 20, No 10, pages 1423-1441.

Bijlmakers, L A, Mary T Bassett and David M Sanders (1998), *Socio-economic Stress, Health and Child Nutrition Status in Zimbabwe at a Time of Economic Structural Adjustment*, Research Report No 105, Nordiska Afrikainstitutet, Uppsala.

Bolnick, Joel (1993), "The People's Dialogue on land and shelter; community-driven networking in South Africa's informal settlements", *Environment and Urbanization*, Vol 5, No 1, April, pages 91-110.

Bolnick, Joel (1996), "uTshani Buyakhuluma (The grass speaks); People's Dialogue and the South African Homeless People's Federation, 1993-1996", *Environment and Urbanization*, Vol 8, No 2, October, pages 153-170.

Boonyabancha, Somsook (2001), "Savings and loans – drawing lessons from some experiences in Asia", *Environment and Urbanization*, Vol 13, No 2, October, pages 9-21.

Boonyabancha, Somsook (2003), *A Decade of Change: from the Urban Community Development Office (UCDO) to the Community Organizations Development Institute (CODI) in Thailand*, IIED Working Paper 12 on Poverty Reduction in Urban Areas, IIED, London, 31 pages.

Boonyabancha, Somsook (2004), "The Urban Community Development Office: increasing community options through a national government development programme in Thailand" in Diana Mitlin and David Satterthwaite (editors), *Empowering Squatter Citizen*, Earthscan Publications, London.

Burkina Faso, Government of (2000), *Poverty Reduction Strategy Paper*, Ministry of Economy and Finance, Ouagadougou, 82 pages.

Burra, Sundar, Sheela Patel and Tom Kerr (2003), "Community-designed, built and managed toilet blocks in Indian cities", *Environment and Urbanization*, Vol 15, No 2, October, pages 11-32.

Cain, Allan, Mary Daly and Paul Robson (2002), *Basic Service Provision for the Urban Poor; the Experience of Development Workshop in Angola*, IIED Working Paper 8 on Poverty Reduction in Urban Areas, IIED, London, 40 pages.

Cairncross, Sandy (1990), "Water supply and the urban poor" in Jorge E Hardoy, Sandy Cairncross and David Satterthwaite (editors), *The Poor Die Young: Housing and Health in Third World Cities*, Earthscan Publications, London, pages 109-126.

Cairncross, Sandy, Jorge E Hardoy and David Satterthwaite (1990), "The urban context" in Jorge E Hardoy, Sandy Cairncross and David Satterthwaite (editors), *The Poor Die Young: Housing and Health in Third World Cities*, Earthscan Publications, London, pages 1-24.

Cambodia, Kingdom of (2002), *National Poverty Reduction Strategy*, Council for Social Development, Phnom Penh, 238 pages.

Cameroon, Republic of, (2002), *Living Conditions and Poverty Profile in Cameroon in 2001: Final Results*, Bureau of Statistics and National Accounts Ministry of Economy and Finance, Republic of Cameroon, 115 pages, downloaded from http://www4.worldbank.org/afr/poverty/databank/docnav/default.cfm.

CARE/Bangladesh (1998), *Urban Livelihood Security Assessment in Bangladesh, Volume 1: Main Report*, edited by Phil Sutter and Chris Perine, 80 pages.

Cavalcanti, Débora, Olinda Marques and Teresa Hilda Costa (2004), "Municipal programme for the reform and extension of homes: Casa Melhor/PAAC Cearah Periferia – Brazil" in Diana Mitlin and David Satterthwaite (editors), *Empowering Squatter Citizen*, Earthscan Publications, London.

Chad, Republic of (2003), *National Poverty Reduction Strategy Paper*, PRSP Steering Committee, Ministry of Planning, Development and Cooperation, N'Djamena

Chambers, Robert (1995), "Poverty and livelihoods; whose reality counts?", *Environment and Urbanization*, Vol 7, No 1, April, pages 173-204.

Champetier, Séverine and Mohamed Farid (2000), *Independent Water and Sanitation Providers in Africa: Nairobi, Kenya, Case Study 5*, Water and Sanitation Program - East and Southern Africa, Nairobi, 8 pages.

Champetier, Séverine, Adam Sykes and Bill Wandera (2000), *Independent Water and Sanitation Providers in Africa: Dar es Salaam, Tanzania, Case Study 10*, Water and Sanitation Program - East and Southern Africa, Nairobi, 6 pages.

Champetier, Séverine and Bill Wandera (2000), *Independent Water and Sanitation Providers in Africa: Kampala, Uganda, Case Study 8*, Water and Sanitation Program - East and Southern Africa, Nairobi, 6 pages.

Chenery, Hollis, Montek S Ahluwalia, C G L Bell, John H Duloy and Richard Jolly (1974), *Redistribution with Growth*, Oxford University Press.

Chitekwe, Beth and Diana Mitlin (2001), "The urban poor under threat and in struggle: options for urban development in Zimbabwe, 1995-2000", *Environment and Urbanization*, Vol 13, No 2, October, pages 85-101.

Citro, C and R Michael (1995), *Measuring Poverty: a New Approach*, National Research Council, National Academy Press, Washington DC.

CODI (2004), *CODI Update 4*, CODI, Bangkok, June, 32 pages.

COHRE (1994), "The Centre on Housing Rights and Evictions (COHRE)", *Environment and Urbanization*, Vol 6, No 1, April, pages 147-157.

Connolly, Priscilla (2004), "The Mexican National Popular Housing Fund (FONHAPO)" in Diana Mitlin and David Satterthwaite (editors), *Empowering Squatter Citizen*, Earthscan Publications, London.

Côte d'Ivoire, Republique de la (2000*), Profil et determinants de la pauvreté en Côte d'Ivoire en 1998*, Institut National de la Statistique, Abidjan, 112 pages.

Coulomb, H and A McKay (1995), *An Assessment of Trends in Poverty in Ghana: 1988-92*, PSP Discussion Paper 81, World Bank, Washington DC.

Cuenya, Beatriz, Diego Armus, Maria Di Loreto and Susana Penalva (1990), "Land invasions and grassroots organization: the Quilmes settlement in Greater Buenos Aires, Argentina", *Environment and Urbanization*, Vol 2, No 1, April, pages 61-73.

Cuenya, Beatriz, Hector Almada, Diego Armus, Julia Castells, Maria di Loreto and Susana Penalva (1990), "Housing and health problems in Buenos Aires – the case of Barrio San Martin" in Sandy Cairncross,

48

Jorge E Hardoy and David Satterthwaite (editors), *The Poor Die Young: Housing and Health in Third World Cities*, Earthscan Publications, London.

Datt, Gaurav and Dean Jolliffe (1999), *Determinants of Poverty in Egypt: 1997*, FCND Discussion Paper No 75, IFPRI, Washington DC.

Deaton, Angus and Christina Paxson (1995), *Measuring Poverty Among the Elderly*, NBER Working Paper 5296, National Bureau of Economic Research, Cambridge, Mass, USA.

Deaton, Angus and Alessandro Tarozzi (2000), *Prices and Poverty in India*, Research Program in Development Studies, Princeton University, Princeton, 54 pages.

Deaton, Angus and Salman Zaidi (2002), *Guidelines for Constructing Consumption Aggregates for Welfare Analysis*, LSMS Working Paper 135, World Bank, Washington DC, 104 pages.

Devas, Nick and David Korboe (2000), "City governance and poverty: the case of Kumasi", *Environment and Urbanization*, Vol 12, No 1, pages 123-135.

Dinye, Romanus D (1995), "A gender sensitive situation analysis of the urban poor, a case study in Kumasi, Ghana", *Trialog*, Vol 44, pages 34-37.

Environment and Urbanization (1989), "Beyond the stereotype of slums; how the poor find accommodation in Third World Cities", Editorial, Vol 1, No 2, October, pages 2-15.

Environment and Urbanization (1995), "The under-estimation and misrepresentation of urban poverty" Editorial, Vol 7, No 1, April, pages 3-10.

Environment and Urbanization (1995), "Urban poverty – from understanding to action", Editorial, Vol 7, No 2, October, pages 3-10.

Etemadi, Felisa U (2000), "Civil society participation in city governance in Cebu City", *Environment and Urbanization*, Vol 12, No 1, April, pages 57-72.

Fay, Marianne and Charlotte Opal (2000), *Urbanization without Growth:A not so uncommon Phenomenon*, World Bank, Washington DC, 31 pages.

Feres, Juan Carlos and Arturo Leon (1990), "The magnitude of poverty in Latin America", *CEPAL Review*, No 41, August, pages 133-151.

Gambia, Republic of (2002), *Strategy for Poverty Alleviation (SPAII)*, PRSP, Department of State for Finance and Economic Affairs.

Ghana, Government of (2000), *Poverty Trends in Ghana in the 1990s*, Ghana Statistical Services, Accra, 70 pages, downloaded from http://www4.worldbank.org/afr/poverty/databank/docnav/default.cfm.

Ghana, Government of (2001), *Core Welfare Indicators Questionnaire (CWIQ) Survey 1997*, CWIQ Regional Profiles, Statistical Service, Government of Ghana, Accra, 110 pages.

Ghosh, A, S S Ahmad and Shipra Maitra (1994), *Basic Services for Urban Poor: A Study of Baroda, Bhilwara, Sambalpur and Siliguri*, Urban Studies Series No 3, Institute of Social Sciences and Concept Publishing Company, New Delhi, 305 pages.

Glockner, Heike, Meki Mkanga and Timothy Ndezi (2004), "Local empowerment through community mapping processes in Tanzania", *Environment and Urbanization*, Vol 16, No 1, April, pages 185-198.

Good, Kenneth (1999), "The state and extreme poverty in Botswana: the San and destitutes", *The Journal of Modern African Studies*, Vol 37, No 2, pages 185-205.

GHK and IIED (2004), *China Urban Poverty Study*, Prepared for the UK Government's Department for International Development, GHK Hong Kong.

Grewe, Christopher and Charles E Becker (forthcoming), *Characteristics of Poor Households in Indonesia*, Background Paper for the Panel on Urban Population Dynamics, Committee on Population. National Research Council/National Academy of Sciences.

Grootaert, Christiaan (1996), *Analysing Poverty and Policy Reform: The Experience of Côte d'Ivoire*, Avebury, Aldershot, Hants, England; Brookfield, Vt. USA, 198 pages.

Haddad, Lawrence, John Hoddinott and Harold Alderman (editors) (1997), *Intrahousehold Resource Allocation in Developing Countries; Methods, Models, and Policy*, The Johns Hopkins University Press, Baltimore, 358 pages.

Haddad, Lawrence, Marie Ruel and James Garrett (1999), "Are urban poverty and undernutrition growing? Some newly assembled evidence", *World Development*, Vol 27, No 11, pages 1891-1904.

Hardoy, Jorge E and David Satterthwaite (1989*), Squatter Citizen: Life in the Urban Third World*, Earthscan Publications, London, 388 pages.

Hardoy, Jorge E Diana Mitlin and David Satterthwaite (2001), *Environmental Problems in an Urbanizing World: Finding Solutions for Cities in Africa, Asia and Latin America*, Earthscan Publications, London, 470 pages.

Hasan, Arif (1997), *Working with Government: The Story of the Orangi Pilot Project's Collaboration with State Agencies for Replicating its Low-cost Sanitation Programme*, City Press, Karachi, 269 pages.

Hasan, Arif (1999), *Understanding Karachi: Planning and Reform for the Future*, City Press, Karachi, 171 pages.

Hentschel, J and Peter Lanjouw (1996), *Constructing an Indicator for Consumption for the Analysis of Poverty*, LSMS Working Paper No 124, World Bank, Washington DC, 40 pages.

Herzer, Hilda, María Mercedes Di Virgilio, Máximo Lanzetta, María Carla Rodríguez and Adriana Redondo (2000), "The formation of social organizations and their attempts to consolidate settlements undergoing transition in Buenos Aires, Argentina", *Environment and Urbanization*, Vol 12, No 1, April, pages 215-230.

Huq, A T, M Zahurul and Borhan Uddin (1996), "Transport and the urban poor" in Nazrul Islam (editor) *The Urban Poor in Bangladesh*, Centre for Urban Studies, Dhaka, 123 pages.

ILO (1976), *Employment, Growth and Basic Needs: A One World Problem*, International Labour Office, Geneva.

Islam, Nazrul, Nurul Huda, Francis B. Narayan and Pradumna B. Rana (eds.) (1997), *Addressing the Urban Poverty Agenda in Bangladesh, Critical Issues and the 1995 Survey Findings*, The University Press Limited, Dhaka, 323 pages.

Jenkins, Paul (2000), "Urban management, urban poverty and urban governance: planning and land management in Maputo, Mozambique, *Environment and Urbanization*, Vol 12, No 1, pages 137-152.

Jonsson, Åsa and David Satterthwaite (2000), *Income-based poverty lines; how well do the levels set internationally and within each country reflect (a) the cost of living in the larger/more prosperous/more expensive cities; and (b) the cost that the urban,* Paper prepared for the Panel on Urban Population Dynamics, Committee on Population, National Research Council/National Academy of Sciences, Washington DC, 63 pages.

Kanbur, Ravi and Lyn Squire (2001) "The evolution of thinking about poverty: exploring the interactions" in Meier, Gerald M and Joseph E Stiglitz, *Frontiers of Development Economics; the Future in Perspective*, Oxford University Press, pages 183-226.

Kanji, Nazneen (1995), "Gender, poverty and structural adjustment in Harare, Zimbabwe", *Environment and Urbanization*, Vol 7, No 1, April, pages 37-55.

Katui-Katua, Munguti and Gordon McGranahan (2002), *Small Enterprises and Water Provision in Kibera, Nairobi, Public Private Partnerships and the Poor*, Water, Engineering and Development Centre (WEDC), Loughborough, 38 pages.

Kenya, Government of (2000), *Poverty in Kenya*, Human Resources and Social Services Department and Central Bureau of Statistics, Ministry of Finance and Planning, Nairobi, 39 pages, downloaded from http://www4.worldbank.org/afr/poverty/databank/docnav/default.cfm.

Khusro, A M (1999), *The Poverty of Nations*, Macmillan, Baskingtoke.

Kironde, J M Lusugga (1995), "Access to land by the urban poor in Tanzania: some findings from Dar es Salaam", *Environment and Urbanization*, Vol 7, No 1, April, pages 77-95.

Kwon, Soon-Won (1998), "National profile of poverty" in UNDP, *Combating Poverty: the Korean Experience*, United Nations Development Programme (UNDP), Seoul.

Lamba, Davinder (1994), "The forgotten half: environmental health in Nairobi's poverty areas", *Environment and Urbanization*, Vol 6, No 1, April, pages 164-173.

Lanjouw, Jean Olson (1998), *Demystifying Poverty Lines*, Poverty Elimination Programme, UNDP, New York, 28 pages, downloaded from http://www.undp.org/seped/index.htm

Lanjouw, Peter, Giovanna Prennushi and Salman Zaidi (1999), "Poverty in Nepal today", in Giovanna Prennushi, *Nepal: Poverty at the Turn of the Twenty-First Century, Background Studies*, Report No. IDP 174, The World Bank, Washington DC, pages 1-28.

Latapí, Augustín Escobar and Mercedes González de la Rocha (1995), "Crisis, restructuring and urban poverty in Mexico", *Environment and Urbanization*, Vol 7, No 1, April, pages 57-75.

Lee, Joung-Woo (1998), "Urban poverty" in UNDP, *Combating Poverty: the Korean Experience*, United Nations Development Programme (UNDP), Seoul, pages 119-143.

Leonard, H Jeffrey (1989), "Environment and the poor: development strategies for a common agenda" in H Jeffrey Leonard and contributors, *Environment and the Poor: Development Strategies for a Common Agenda*, Overseas Development Council, Transaction Books, New Brunswick, USA and Oxford, UK, pages 3-45.

Malawi, Government of (1994), *Survey of Household Expenditure and Small-scale Economic Activities 1990/91*, National Statistics Office.

Malawi, Government of (2000), *Profile of Poverty in Malawi, 1998*, Poverty Monitoring System, National Economic Council, Government of Malawi, 110 pages, downloaded from http://www4.worldbank.org/afr/poverty/databank/docnav/default.cfm.

Mauritania, Islamic Republic of (2000), *Poverty Reduction Strategy Paper*, 75 pages.

Maxwell, Dan (1998), *The Political Economy of Urban Food Security in sub-Saharan Africa*, FCND Discussion Papers, International Food Policy Research Institute (IFPRI), Washington DC, 65 pages.

Maxwell, Daniel, Carol Levin, Margaret Armar-Klemesu, Marie Ruel, Saul Morris and Clement Ahiadeke (1998), *Urban Livelihoods and Food and Nutrition Security in Greater Accra, Ghana*, International Food Policy Research Institute (IFPRI), Washington DC.

McGranahan, Gordon, Pedro Jacobi, Jacob Songsore, Charles Surjadi and Marianne Kjellén (2001), *The Citizens at Risk: From Urban Sanitation to Sustainable Cities*, Earthscan Publications, London, 200 pages.

McIntosh, Arthur C and Cesar E Yñiguez (1997), *Second Water Utilities Data Book*, Asian Development Bank, Manila, 210 pages.

Mearns, Robin (2004), "Sustaining livelihoods on Mongolia's pastoral commons: insights from a participatory assessment", *Development and Change*, Vol 35, No. 1, pages 107-139.

Mejía, José Antonio and Rob Vos (1997), *Poverty in Latin America and the Caribbean. An Inventory: 1980-95*, Document prepared in the context of the programme for the "Improvement of Surveys and the Measurement of Living Conditions in Latin America and the Caribbean", co-sponsored by the IDB, World Bank and CEPAL, Working Paper Series I-4.

Minujin, Alberto (1995), "Squeezed: the middle class in Latin America", *Environment and Urbanization*, Vol 7, No 2, October, pages 153-166.

Minujin, Alberto (1999), "Monitoring rights and goals for children", paper presented at the Third Meeting of the Expert group on Poverty Statistics (Rio Group), Lisbon, November.

Misra, Harikesh (1990), "Housing and health problems in three squatter settlements in Allahabad, India" in Sandy Cairncross, Jorge E Hardoy and David Satterthwaite (editors), *The Poor Die Young: Housing and Health in Third World Cities*, Earthscan Publications, London.

Mitlin, Diana (1997), "Building with credit: housing finance for low-income households", *Third World Planning Review*, Vol 19, No 1, London, pages 21-50.

Mitlin, Diana (2004), *Understanding urban poverty; what the Poverty Reduction Strategy Papers tell us*, IIED Working Paper 13 on Poverty Reduction in Urban Areas, IIED, London.

Mitlin, Diana and David Satterthwaite (2001), "Urban poverty: some thoughts about its scale and nature and about responses to it ", Chapter 12 in Shahid Yusuf, Simon Evenett and Weiping Wu (editors), *Facets of Globalization; International and Local Dimensions of Development*, World Bank, Washington DC, pages 193-220.

Mitlin, Diana and David Satterthwaite (editors) (2004), *Empowering Squatter Citizen: Local Government Civil Society and Urban Poverty Reduction*, Earthscan Publications, London, 313 pages.

Montgomery, Mark R, Richard Stren, Barney Cohen and Holly E Reed (editors) (2003), *Cities Transformed; Demographic Change and its Implications in the Developing World*, the National Academy Press, Washington DC, 518 pages.

Moser, Caroline O N (1993), *Urban Social Policy and Poverty Reduction*, TWURD Working Paper # 10, Urban Development Division, World Bank, Washington DC, October, 16 pages.

Moser, Caroline O N (1996), *Confronting Crisis: A Summary of Household Responses to Poverty and Vulnerability in Four Poor urban Communities*, Environmentally Sustainable Development Studies and Monographs Series No 7, The World Bank, Washington DC, 19 pages.

Moser, Caroline O N (1998), "The asset vulnerability framework: reassessing urban poverty reduction strategies", *World Development*, Vol 26, No 1, pages 1-19.

Moser, Caroline O N, Alicia J Herbert and Roza E Makonnen (1993), *Urban Poverty in the Context of Structural Adjustment; Recent Evidence and Policy Responses*, TWU Discussion Paper DP #4, Urban Development Division, World Bank, Washington DC, 140 pages.

Mozambique, Government of, Ministry of Planning and Finance, Eduardo Mondlane University and the International Food Policy Research Institute (IFPRI) (1998), *Understanding Poverty and Well-being in Mozambique: The First National Assessment (1996-97)*.

Mozambique, Republic of (2001), *Action Plan for the Reduction of Absolute Poverty (2001-2005)*, Final version approved by the Council of Ministers, downloaded from the World Bank website.

Mupedziswa, Rodrick and Perpetua Gumbo (1998), *Structural Adjustment and Women Informal Sector Traders in Harare, Zimbabwe*, The Nordic African Institute Research Report 106, 123 pages.

Murphy, Denis and Ted Anana (1994), "Evictions and fear of evictions in the Philippines", *Environment and Urbanization*, Vol 6, No 1, April, pages 40-49.

National Statistical Institute of Portugal (INE) (1999), *Report of the Seminar on Poverty Statistics,* Paper submitted by the Working Group of Statistical Experts for the Third Meeting of the Expert Group on Poverty Statistics, Rio Group, Lisbon, 22-24 November.

Navarro, Lia (2001), "Exploring the environmental and political dimensions of poverty: the cases of the cities of Mar del Plata and Necochea-Quequén", *Environment and Urbanization*, Vol 13, No 1, April, pages 185-199.

Niger, Republique du (2002), *Poverty Reduction Strategy*, Office of the Prime Minister; Permanent Secretariat of the PRSP, Niamey.

Orangi Pilot Project (1995), Orangi Pilot Project, *Environment and Urbanization*, Vol 7, No 2, October, pages 227-236.

Orangi Pilot Project – Research and Training Institute (2002), *Katchi Abadis of Karachi: Documentation of Sewerage, Water Supply Lines, Clinics, Schools and Thallas – Volume One: The First Hundred Katchi Abadis Surveyed*, Orangi Pilot Project, Karachi, 507 pages.

Pamoja Trust (2001), *Huruma Informal Settlements – Planning Survey Report*, Pamoja Trust, Nairobi.

Pakistan, Government of the Islamic Republic of (2001), *Poverty Reduction Partnership Agreement between the Government of the Islamic Republic of Pakistan and the Asian Development Bank*, Asian Development Bank, Manila, 15 pages.

Patel, Sheela (1990), "Street children, hotel boys and children of pavement dwellers and construction workers in Bombay: how they meet their daily needs", *Environment and Urbanization*, Vol 2, No 2, October, pages 9-26.

Patel, Sheela (2004), "Tools and methods for empowerment developed by slum dwellers federations in India", *Participatory Learning and Action 50*, IIED, London.

Patel, Sheela and Celine D'Cruz (1993), "The Mahila Milan crisis credit scheme; from a seed to a tree", *Environment and Urbanization*, Vol 5, No 1, April, pages 9-17.

Patel, Sheela and Diana Mitlin (2001), *The work of SPARC and its partners Mahila Milan and the National Slum Dwellers Federation in India*, IIED Working Paper 5 on Urban Poverty Reduction, IIED, London.

Patel, Sheela, Celine D'Cruz and Sundar Burra (2002), "Beyond evictions in a global city; people-managed resettlement in Mumbai", *Environment and Urbanization*, Vol 14, No 1, April, pages 159-172.

Paternostro, Stefano, Jean Razafindravonona and David Stifel (2001), *Changes in Poverty in Madagascar: 1993-1999*, Africa Region Working Paper Series No. 19, World Bank, Washington DC, 103 pages.

Porio, Emma with the assistance of Christine S Crisol, Nota F Magno, David Cid and Evelyn N Paul (2004), "The Community Mortgage Program (CMP): an innovative social housing programme in the Philippines and its Outcomes" in Diana Mitlin and David Satterthwaite (editors), *Empowering Squatter Citizen*, Earthscan Publications, London.

Prennushi, Giovanna (1999), *Nepal: Poverty at the Turn of the Twenty-First Century; Main Report*, Report No IDP 174, The World Bank, Washington DC, 71 pages.

Potts, Deborah and C C Mutambirwa (1991), "High-density housing in Harare: commodification and overcrowding, *Third World Planning Review*, Vol 13, No 1, pages 1-25.

Pryer, Jane (1993) "The impact of adult ill-health on household income and nutrition in Khulna, Bangladesh", *Environment and Urbanization*, Vol 5, No 2, October, pages 35-49.

Pryer, Jane (2003), *Poverty and Vulnerability in Dhaka Slums; the Urban Livelihoods Study*, Ashgate, Aldershot, Hants, 203 pages.

Rakodi, Carole (1995), "Poverty lines or household strategies? A review of conceptual issues in the study of urban poverty", *Habitat International*, Vol 19, No 4, pages 407-426.

Rakodi, Carole and Penny Withers (1995), "Housing aspirations and affordability in Harare and Gweru, a contribution to housing policy formation in Zimbabwe", *Cities*, Vol 12, No 3, pages 185-201.

Rakodi, Carole with Tony Lloyd-Jones (editors) (2002), *Urban Livelihoods: A People-centred Approach to Reducing Poverty*, Earthscan Publications, London, 306 pages.

Rakodi, Carole, Rose Gatabaki-Kamau and Nick Devas (2000), "Poverty and political conflict in Mombasa", *Environment and Urbanization*, Vol 12, No 1, April, pages 153-170.

Ravallion Martin and Benu Bidani (1994), "How robust is a poverty profile?", *The World Bank Economic Review*, Vol 8, No 1, pages 75-102.

Ravallion, Martin (1998), *Poverty Lines in Theory and Practice*, Living Standards Measurement Study Working Paper No 133, World Bank, Washington DC, 35 pages.

Reddy, Sanjay G and Thomas W Pogge (2003), *How Not to Count the Poor*, Version 4.5, downloaded from http://www.columbia.edu/~sr793/count.pdf, 73 pages.

Richmond, Pattie (1997), "From tenants to owners: experiences with a revolving fund for social housing", *Environment and Urbanization*, Vol 9, No 2, October, pages 119-139.

Rowntree, B. Seebohm (1902), *Poverty: A Study of Town Life*, text of Chapter 5 accessed at http://www2.arts.gla.ac.uk/History/ESH/rowntree/chap5.html where it is reproduced with the permission of the Joseph Rowntree Charitable Trust. This is drawn from the second edition, pages 119-145 (the first edition was 1901).

Ruel, Marie T, James L Garrett, Saul S Morris, David Maxwell, Arne Oshaug, Patrice Engle, Purnima Menon, Alison Slack and Laurence Haddad (1998), *Urban Challenges to Nutrition Security: A Review of Food Security, Health and Care in the Cities*, FCND Discussion Paper No 51, IFPRI, Washington DC.

Ruel, Marie T, James L Garrett and Lawrence Haddad (1999), "Urban challenges to food and nutrition security in the developing world", *World Development*, Vol 27, No 11, November, pages.

Saghir, Jamal, Manuel Schiffler and Mathewos Woldu (2000), *Urban Water and Sanitation in the Middle East and North Africa Region: The Way Forward*, Middle East and North Africa Region Infrastructure Development Group, The World Bank, Washington DC.

Sahn, David E and David C Stifel (2003), "Progress towards the Millennium Development Goals in Africa", *World Development*, Vol 31, No 1, pages 23-52.

Sandbrook, Richard (1982), *The Politics of Basic Needs: Urban Aspects of Assaulting Poverty in Africa*, Heinemann Educational, London.

Satterthwaite, David (1995), "The underestimation of poverty and its health consequences", *Third World Planning Review*, Vol 17, No 4, November, pages iii-xii.

Satterthwaite, David (1997a), "Urban poverty: reconsidering its scale and nature", *IDS Bulletin*, Vol 28, No 2, April, pages 9-23.

Satterthwaite, David (1997b), *The Scale and Nature of International Donor Assistance to Housing, Basic Services and Other Human Settlements-related Projects*, WIDER, Helsinki, 38 pages.

Satterthwaite, David (2001), "Reducing urban poverty: constraints on the effectiveness of aid agencies and development banks and some suggestions for change", *Environment and Urbanization*, Vol 13, No 1, April, pages 137-157.

Satterthwaite, David (2002a), *Coping with Rapid Urban Growth*, RICS International Paper Series, Royal Institution of Chartered Surveyors, London, 35 pages,

Satterthwaite, David (2002b), *Reducing Urban Poverty: Some Lessons From Experience*, Poverty Reduction in Urban Areas Series Working Paper 11, IIED, London, 40 pages.

Satterthwaite, David and Cecilia Tacoli (2002), "Seeking an understanding of poverty that recognizes rural–urban differences and rural-urban linkages" in Carole Rakodi with Tony Lloyd-Jones (editors), *Urban Livelihoods: A People-centred Approach to Reducing Poverty*, Earthscan Publications, London, pages 52-70.

Satterthwaite, David and Cecilia Tacoli (2003), *The Urban Part of Rural Development: The Role of Small and Intermediate Urban Centres in Rural and Regional Development and Poverty Reduction*, Rural-Urban Working Papers Series, No 9, IIED, London, 64 pages.

Schlyter, Ann (1990), *Women Householders and Housing Strategies: the Case of Harare, Zimbabwe*, the National Swedish Institute for Building Research, Stockholm, 203 pages.

Schusterman, Ricardo and Ana Hardoy (1997), "Reconstructing social capital in a poor urban settlement: the Integrated Improvement Programme, Barrio San Jorge", *Environment and Urbanization*, Vol 9, No1, April, pages 91-119.

Schusterman, Ricardo, Florencia Almansi, Ana Hardoy, Cecilia Monti and Gastón Urquiza (2001), *Poverty Reduction in Action: Participatory Planning in San Fernando, Buenos Aires*, IIED Working Paper 6 on Poverty Reduction in Urban Areas, IIED, London.

Senegal, Republic of (2002), *Poverty Reduction Strategy Paper; One People, One Goal, One Faith*, Dakar.

Solo, Tova Maria (2000), *Independent Water Entrepreneurs in Latin America; the Other Private Sector in Water Services*, Draft, World Bank, Washington DC.

Songsore, Jacob and Gordon McGranahan (1993), "Environment, wealth and health; towards an analysis of intra-urban differentials within Greater Accra Metropolitan Area, Ghana", *Environment and Urbanization*, Vol 5, No 2, October, pages 10-24.

South Africa, Government of (1995), *Key Indicators of Poverty in South Africa*, Ministry in the Office of the President, Reconstruction and Development Programme, Pretoria, 27 pages.

SPARC (1985), *"We the Invisible"; a Census of Pavement Dwellers*, Bombay, 41 pages.

Sri Lanka, Government of (2002), *Regaining Sri Lanka: Vision and Strategy for Accelerated Development*, 222 pages.

Stein, Alfredo (2001), *Participation and sustainability in social projects: the experience of the Local Development Programme (PRODEL) in Nicaragua*, IIED Working Paper 3 on Poverty Reduction in Urban Areas, IIED, London.

Streeten, Paul (1981), *First Things First – Meeting Basic Needs in Developing Countries*, Oxford University Press.

Swaminathan, Madhura (1995), "Aspects of urban poverty in Bombay, *Environment and Urbanization*, Vol 7, No 1, April, pages 133-143.

Swaziland, Kingdom of (1998), *Welfare and Poverty in Swaziland; 1985-95*, World Bank, AFT11, Washington DC, 57 pages.

Tabatabai, Hamid with Manal Fouad (1993), *The Incidence of Poverty in Developing Countries; an ILO Compendium of Data*, a World Employment Programme Study, International Labour Office, Geneva, 105 pages.

Tacoli, Cecilia (1998), *Bridging the Divide: Rural–Urban Interactions and Livelihood Strategies*, Gatekeeper Series No 77, IIED Sustainable Agriculture and Rural Livelihoods Programme, London, 17 pages.

Tanzania, Government of (2002a), *Tanzania: Poverty and Human Development Report (draft)*, Research and Analysis Working Group (R&AWG) Bureau of Statistics, Dar es Salaam, 119 pages, downloaded from http://www4.worldbank.org/afr/poverty/databank/docnav/default.cfm.

Tanzania, Government of (2002b), *Household Budget Survey 2000/2001: Tanzania*, National Bureau of Statistics, Tanzania, Dar es Salaam, 220 pages, downloaded from http://www4.worldbank.org/afr/poverty/databank/docnav/default.cfm.

Tchad, République du (2001), *Enquête par grappes à indicateurs multiples: Rapport complet*, Bureau Central de Recensement, Ministère de la Promotion Economique et du Développement, 107 pages, downloaded from http://www4.worldbank.org/afr/poverty/databank/docnav/default.cfm

Thomas, EP, JR Seager, E Viljoen, F Potgieter, A Rossouw, B Tokota, G McGranahan and M Kjellen (1999), *Household Environment and Health in Port Elizabeth, South Africa*, Urban Environment Series Report No 6, Stockholm Environment Institute in collaboration with South African Medical Research Council, Stockholm, 126 pages.

Thompson, John, Ina T Porras, Elisabeth Wood, James K Tumwine, Mark R Mujwahuzi, Munguti Katui-Katua and Nick Johnstone (2000), "Waiting at the tap: Changes in urban water use in East Africa over three decades", *Environment and Urbanization*, Vol 12, No 2, pages 37-52. .

Turner, John F C (1976), *Housing By People – Towards Autonomy in Building Environments*, Ideas in Progress, Marion Boyars, London.

UNCHS (1993), *Support Measures to Promote Rental Housing for Low-income Groups*, United Nations Centre for Human Settlements, HS/294/93E, Nairobi.

UNCHS (1996), *An Urbanizing World: Global Report on Human Settlements, 1996*, Oxford University Press, Oxford and New York.

UNCHS and World Bank (1993), *The Housing Indicators Program Volume III; Preliminary Findings*, a Joint Programme of the United Nations Centre for Human Settlements (Habitat) and the World Bank, Washington DC.

UNDP (United Nations Development Programme) (1998), *Combating Poverty: the Korean Experience*, UNDP, Seoul.

UN–Habitat (2003a), *Water and Sanitation in the World's Cities: Local Action for Global Goals*, Earthscan Publications, London.

UN–Habitat (2003b), *The Challenge of Slums: Global Report on Human Settlements 2003*, Earthscan Publications, London.

UNICEF (2000), *Progotir Pathey; On the Road to Progress; Achieving the Goals for Children in Bangladesh*, Bangladesh Bureau of Statistics and UNICEF, Dhaka, 122 pages.

United Nations (2002), *World Urbanization Prospects; the 2001 Revision*, Population Division, Department of Economic and Social Affairs, United Nations, ST/ESA/SER.A/216, New York, 321 pages.

URC (1994), The Urban Resource Centre, Karachi, *Environment and Urbanization*, Vol 6, No 1, April, pages 158-163.

URC (Urban Resource Centre) (2001), "Urban poverty and transport: a case study from Karachi", *Environment and Urbanization*, Vol 13, No 1, April, pages 223-234.

Velasquez, Luz Stella (1998), "Agenda 21; a form of joint environmental management in Manizales, Colombia", *Environment and Urbanization*, Vol 10, No 2, October, pages 9-36.

Vietnam, Socialist Republic of (2002), *The Comprehensive Poverty Reduction and Growth Strategy*, Hanoi, 139 pages, downloaded from http://www.worldbank.org.vn/

VMSDFI; Vincentian Missionaries Social Development Foundation Incorporated (VMSDFI) (2001), "Meet the Philippines Homeless People's Federation", *Environment and Urbanization*, Vol 13, No 2, October, pages 73-84.

Ward, Barbara (1976), *The Home of Man*, W W Norton, New York.

Water and Sanitation Program (2000), *Independent Water and Sanitation Providers in Africa; Beyond Facts and Figures*, WSP Africa Regional Office, World Bank, Nairobi.

Weru, Jane (2004), "Understanding what community federations bring to city upgrading strategies; the work of Pamoja Trust and Muungano in Kenya", *Environment and Urbanization*, Vol 16, No 1, April, pages 47-62.

WHO (1992), *Our Planet, Our Health*, Report of the WHO Commission on Health and Environment, World Health Organization, Geneva, 282 pages.

WHO (1999), "Creating healthy cities in the 21st Century", Chapter 6 in David Satterthwaite (editor), *The Earthscan Reader on Sustainable Cities*, Earthscan Publications, London, 472 pages.

WHO and UNICEF (2000), *Global Water Supply and Sanitation Assessment, 2000 Report*, World Health Organization, UNICEF and Water Supply and Sanitation Collaborative Council, 80 pages.

Wodon, Quentin T (2000), *Poverty and Policy in Latin America and the Caribbean*, World Bank Technical Paper No 467, World Bank, Washington DC.

World Bank (1990), *World Development Report – 1990; Poverty*, Oxford University Press, Oxford.

World Bank (1991), *Urban Policy and Economic Development: an Agenda for the 1990s*, World Bank, Washington DC, 87 pages.

World Bank (1995), *Kenya Poverty Assessment*, Report No 13152-KE.

World Bank (1996a), *Togo: Overcoming the Crisis, Overcoming Poverty*, a World Bank Poverty Assessment, Population and Human Resources Operations Division, Africa Region, the World Bank, Washington DC, 170 pages, downloaded from http://www4.worldbank.org/afr/poverty/databank/docnav/default.cfm.

World Bank (1996b), *Understanding Poverty and Human Resources in Zimbabwe: Changes in the 1990s and Directions for the Future*, Discussion Paper, Human Development Group, Eastern and Southern Africa, the World Bank, Washington DC, downloaded from http://www4.worldbank.org/afr/poverty/databank/docnav/default.cfm.

World Bank (1998a), *Haiti: the Challenges of Poverty Reduction Volumes I and II*, Report No 17242-HA, Poverty Reduction and Economic Management Unit and Caribbean Country Management Unit, Latin America and the Caribbean Region, World Bank, Washington DC, downloaded from

54

http://wbln0018.worldbank.org/LAC/LAC.nsf/ECADocByUnid/88DC936A5710B68785256C7E00740CBE?Opendocument

World Bank (1998b), *Poverty Profile for Nigeria, 1985-1996*, World Bank, Washington DC, 31 pages.

World Bank (1999a), *Ethiopia: Poverty and Policies for the New Millennium*, Report No 19804-ET, Country Department 6, Africa Region, World Bank, Washington DC, 90 pages, downloaded from http://www4.worldbank.org/afr/poverty/databank/docnav/default.cfm.

World Bank (1999b), *Entering the 21st Century: World Development Report 1999/2000*, Oxford University Press, Oxford and New York, 300 pages.

World Bank (1999c), *Panama Poverty Report*, World Bank, Washington DC, downloaded from http://wbln0018.worldbank.org/LAC/

World Bank (2000), *World Development Report 2000/2001: Attacking Poverty*, Oxford University Press, Oxford and New York, 355 pages.

World Bank (2001a), *Uruguay: Maintaining Social Equity in a Changing Economy*, Report No 21262, Argentina, Chile, Paraguay and Uruguay Country Management Unit, PREM Sector Management Unit, Latin America and the Caribbean Region, World Bank, Washington DC, downloaded from http://wbln0018.worldbank.org/LAC/

World Bank (2001b), *Honduras Poverty Diagnostic 2000*, Poverty Reduction and Economic Management Sector Unit, Latin America and the Caribbean Region, World Bank, Washington DC, downloaded from http://wbln0018.worldbank.org/

World Bank (2001c), *Nicaragua Poverty Assessment: Challenges and Opportunities for Poverty Reduction, Volume I: Main Report*, Report No 20488 NI, Poverty Reduction and Economic Management Sector Unit, Latin America and the Caribbean Region, World Bank, Washington DC, downloaded from http://wbln0018.worldbank.org/lac/

World Bank (2002a), *Philippines Country Assistance Strategy*, Report No 24042-PH, Philippines Country Management Unit, East Asia and Pacific Region, World Bank, Washington DC.

World Bank (2002b), *Poverty in Bangladesh: Building on Progress*, Poverty Reduction and Economic Management Sector Unit, South Asia Region, World Bank and Asian Development Bank, Washington DC, 115 pages, downloaded from http://lnweb18.worldbank.org/SAR/sa.nsf

World Bank (2002c), *Poverty and Social Developments in Peru 1994-1997*, Washington DC, downloaded from http://wbln0018.worldbank.org/lac/

World Bank (2003a), *Guatemala Poverty Assessment*, Poverty Reduction and Economic Management Unit, Human Development Sector Management Unit, Latin America and the Caribbean Region, Report No 24221-GU, World Bank, Washington DC, downloaded from http://wbln0018.worldbank.org/LAC/

Wratten, Ellen (1995), "Conceptualizing urban poverty", *Environment and Urbanization*, Vol 7, No 1, April, pages 11-36.

Wust, Sébastien, Jean-Claude Bolay and Thai Thi Ngoc Du (2002), "Metropolization and the ecological crisis: precarious settlements in Ho Chi Minh City, Vietnam", *Environment and Urbanization*, Vol 14, No 2, October, pages 211-224.

Yapi-Diahou, Alphonse, "The informal housing sector of the metropolis of Abidjan, Ivory Coast", *Environment and Urbanization*, Vol 7, No.2, October, 1995, pages 11-29.

Yemen, Republic of (2002), *Poverty Reduction Strategy Paper*, 2003-2005, 142 pages.

Zambia, Republic of (2002), *Zambia Poverty Reduction Strategy Paper 2002-2004*, Ministry of Finance and National Planning, Lusaka, March.

Zimbabwe, Government of (1998), *Poverty in Zimbabwe*, Central Statistical Office, Harare, 95 pages, downloaded from http://www4.worldbank.org/afr/poverty/databank/docnav/default.cfm.

Annex 1: Examples in the different bases used for setting poverty lines and whether or not allowances were made for differences between rural and urban areas

Nation	Basis for poverty line(s)	Notes	Differences in rural and urban poverty lines?	
Bangladesh (1995)	Price of minimum calorie intake (2,112 kcal) plus 25 percent. Also a lower poverty line for 'hard core' poor with much less for food (only 1,805 kcal) and for non-food items.	An assumption that non-food costs would be 25 percent of food costs.		Islam et al (1997)
Bangladesh (2000)	Food costs based on a food bundle providing minimal nutritional requirements (2,122 kcal per person per day). Adjustment for non-food needs based on average amount spent on non-food items by households. For lower poverty line this was households whose total consumption was equal to the food poverty line; for upper poverty line this was households whose food consumption was equal to the food poverty line.	Separate upper and lower poverty lines for different rural and urban areas.	Prices adjusted for differences between regions.	World Bank (2002b)
Burkina Faso (1998)	The poverty line appears to be set based only on the cost of a calorie intake of 2,300/person/day (approximately CFAF 72,690 per adult per year).			Burkina Faso, Government of (2000)
Cambodia (1999)	Two poverty lines: food poverty line with no allowance for non-food needs; and an overall poverty line with some allowance for non-food needs.	Overall poverty line as a proportion of the food poverty line: 1.42 times for Phnom Penh, 1.32 for other urban and 1.29 for rural.	The overall poverty line for Phnom Penh was 1.39 times that for rural areas. For other urban areas, it was 1.18 times that of rural areas.	Cambodia, Kingdom of (2002)
Cameroon (2001)	The poverty line is set at 232,547 CFA francs per adult equivalent per year. *"This level of spending allows an adult to eat and take care of his/her essential needs at the same time."* 151,398 CFA francs was for food (based on a basket of food goods drawing on consumption data for the 4th to the 7th 10th percentiles to allow an adult to reach 2,900 calories per day). The non-nutritional baseline was calculated based on what the poor who are right at the poverty line spend on non-food items.	The actual poverty line was 1.54 times the food poverty line. Equivalence scales used in transfer of household data to individual data.	It seems as if the same poverty lines are used in both rural and urban areas, although the text emphasizes the price disparities between different regions and some adjustments were made when comparing household consumption using a spatial cost of living index.	Cameroon, Government of (2002)
Chad (1995/6)	Two poverty lines; a food poverty line based on 2,095 calories per person per day for urban areas and 2,175 for rural areas; and an overall poverty line which has some allowance for "minimum non-food	The overall poverty line was 1.33 times the food poverty line for N'Djamena and 1.30 times the food poverty line for other urban centres.	Food-related and overall poverty lines adjusted upwards for N'Djamena and for other towns in comparison to rural areas.	Chad, Republic of (2003)

	consumption needs".		
China (1998/99)	There is no official urban poverty line. A study by the Asian Development Bank used a food-poverty line and a general poverty line	The general poverty line was 1.66 times the food poverty line nationally (although the ratio varied by province from 1.54 to 1.96)	Food poverty lines and poverty lines varied by province; for instance the poverty line for Shanghai province was 1.57 times that of the national line; for Beijing it was 1.35; for Tianjin 1.30.	GHK and IIED (2004), drawing on ADB (2004)
Ethiopia (1995/96)	Two poverty lines: food poverty line (expenditure needed per adult to obtain 2,200 calories a day); and total poverty line (food poverty line plus allowance for non-food items based on share of non-food consumption in total consumption of poorest half of the distribution).	The total poverty line was 1.78 times the food poverty line in urban areas. In 1995/96, the urban and rural total poverty lines were much less than US$ 1 a day; for rural areas, it was US$ 0.43; for urban areas, US$ 0.51.	Allowance made for higher costs in urban areas; the food poverty line was 10 percent higher in urban areas than in rural areas; the total poverty line was 19 percent higher in urban areas than in rural areas.	World Bank (1999a)
Gambia (1998)	Two poverty lines: overall poverty line (cost of a basket of food and some allowance for non-food essentials); and food poverty line (cost of a basket of food).	Overall poverty line 1.66 times the food poverty line (extreme poverty).	As the costs of both food and other items varies considerably between Banjul, other urban centres and rural areas, poverty lines are estimated separately for each area.	Gambia, Republic of (2002)
Ghana (1998/99)	Two poverty lines: extreme poverty (based on income needed to meet nutritional requirements); and upper poverty line (food poverty line plus a small additional amount based on the expenditure devoted to non-food items of those whose total consumption expenditure is at the level of the food poverty line).	Upper poverty line 1.29 times the extreme poverty line.	Adjustments made for different prices between regions for food, housing and other non-food items.	Ghana, Government of (2000)
Guatemala (2000)	Two poverty lines: an extreme poverty line based on the cost of a food basket providing a minimum daily calorie requirement of 2,172 (the basket based on average consumption patterns for entire population); and a full poverty line, with an allowance for non-food needs calculated as the average non-food budget share for the population whose food consumption was around the extreme poverty line.	The full poverty line is 2.26 times the extreme poverty line (Q 4,319 compared to Q 1912).	The same poverty lines used in both rural and urban areas.	World Bank (2003a)
Haiti (1995)	The poverty line is based on the local cost of reaching a minimum standard of 2,240 calories with a diet that matches the average sample household's expenditure on food, plus expenditures on non-food commodities, such that the percentage of food expenditures of total expenditures matches the average for the poorest 72 percent of rural	No figures given for the proportion of the urban population who are below the poverty line; data for determining the poverty line drawn from rural livelihood sample.	The same poverty lines used in both rural and urban areas. Strong stress on the fact that most poverty is in rural areas, although details also given of very poor living conditions in Port-au-Prince and other urban centres.	World Bank (1998a)

Country/Study	Description	Notes	Source
	households; equivalent to G 3321 (US$ 220).		
Honduras (1999)	Two poverty lines: extreme poverty line based on the cost of a food basket designed to meet basic nutritional needs (based on 2,200 kcal per person per day); and moderate poverty line which takes into account basic non-food needs.	In March 1999, the moderate poverty line was 1.68 times the extreme poverty line.	World Bank (2001b)
India – study of four urban centres (1992)	The income level at which urban households typically meet their daily intake of 2,100 calories.	Assumption that households who are managing to meet their daily calorie needs have 'enough income' for non-food needs.	Ghosh et al (1994)
Ivory Coast (1998)	Two poverty lines: the extreme poverty line (95,700 CFA francs in 1998); and the poverty line (162,800 CFA francs in 1998).	The poverty line was 1.7 times the extreme poverty line.	Côte d'Ivoire, République de la (2000)
Kenya (1997)	Three poverty lines: hardcore poor (whose total expenditure was less than the cost of 2,250 calories per adult per day); food poor (where expenditure on food was less than the minimum calorie requirement); and absolute poor (with allowance for non-food needs based on mean non-food household spending for households around the food poverty line).	Absolute poverty line 2.1 times the food poverty line in urban areas.	Kenya, Government of (2000)
Latin America (1996)	Two poverty lines applied across 12 nations: extreme poverty line based on cost of country-specific food baskets providing 2,200 kcal per person per day; and moderate poverty line, set at 1.75 the extreme poverty line for rural areas and 2.0 for urban areas.	'Moderate' poverty line 2.0 times the food poverty line in urban areas.	Wodon (2000)
Madagascar (1999)	Two poverty lines: lower poverty line (extreme poor) based on income just able to purchase the minimum food basket; and upper poverty line with an allowance for 'minimum non-food needs'	Upper poverty line is 1.21 times the lower poverty line.	Paternostro, Razafindravonona and Stifel (2001)
Malawi (1997/98)	Two poverty lines: the poverty line based on the costs for a poor household of acquiring sufficient calories and a non-food component based on households whose total consumption and expenditure is close to the value of the food component of the poverty line; and the ultra poverty line which is 60 percent of the poverty line.	Poverty line is 1.5 times the allowance made for food in urban areas.	Malawi, Government of (2000)
		Adjustment for different costs in four regions, one of which is the main urban centres. In 1998, the urban poverty line was 2.27-3.27 times that of the rural regions.	

Country (year)	Poverty line description	Rural/urban adjustment	Source
Mauritania (1996)	Two poverty lines: extreme poverty and poverty.	No adjustment made for poverty lines for rural and urban areas; strong stress on how rural poverty is much greater and more serious than urban poverty.	Mauritania, Islamic Republic of (2000)
Mongolia (1998)	For the poverty line, the food component is the minimum required dietary intake based on actual average consumption pattern of the poorest 40 percent of households. The allowance for non-food expenditures is based on what is spent on non-food items households whose total expenditure is equal to the amount needed to purchase the minimum food basket	The documentation noted that "*A poverty threshold specific to Mauritania has not yet been calculated*"; the poverty line was based on a US$ 1 a day poverty line and was 1.32 times the extreme poverty line.	Mearns (2004)
Mozambique (1996/97)	Absolute poverty line: sum of the food poverty line based on nutritional standards of approx 2,150 calories a day plus a modest amount of non-food expenditure based on consumption by households that suffer from food insecurity. Destitution/abject poverty line based on those who were unable to satisfy their daily calorie requirement (60 percent of the base poverty line).	Absolute poverty line 1.66 times the food poverty line.	There are adjustments made for different living costs by province, but no details of their scale.	Mozambique, Republic of (2001)
Nepal (1995/6)	Absolute poverty line based on 2,124 calories per person per day with the food basket based on food items consumed by Nepali households in the second to fifth decile of per capita consumption distribution plus an allowance for non-food items based on the non-food expenditures of households whose spending on food was enough to meet their minimum food requirements.	Absolute poverty line was 1.67 times the food poverty line.	Adjustments made for different living costs between Kathmandu, other urban and four rural regions based on differences in food prices and housing prices (estimated). No price data were available for non-food items.	Prennushi 1999, Lanjouw, Prennushi and Zaidi 1999
Nicaragua (1998)	Two poverty lines: extreme poverty line based on the cost of meeting a daily calorie requirement of 2,226; and general poverty line, with an allowance for non-food needs.	General poverty line 1.9 times the extreme poverty line.	No adjustments made for urban; strong stress on "*…poverty and extreme poverty remaining overwhelmingly rural*".	World Bank (2001c)
Niger (1993)	Poverty line and extreme poverty line (set at around two-thirds of the poverty line); not clear how the poverty line was set.	Poverty line 1.5 times the extreme poverty line.	Urban poverty line set at 1.5 times that of the rural poverty line.	Niger, République du (2002)

Country (year)	Poverty line definition	Relationship	Allowance for urban/rural variation	Source
Nigeria (1996/7)	Two poverty lines: the moderate poverty line equivalent to two-thirds of the mean per capita expenditure; and the core poverty line equivalent to one-third of mean capital expenditure.	Moderate poverty line twice the core poverty line.	No allowance made for variations in costs between rural and urban areas.	Nigeria (1998b)
Panama (1997)	Two poverty lines: extreme poverty line based on the level of per capita annual consumption (income) required to satisfy the minimum average daily calorie requirement of 2,280 kcal; and a full poverty line based on extreme poverty line plus an allowance for non-food needs based on non-food budget share of those individuals with total consumption that is close to the extreme poverty line.	Full poverty line 1.74 times higher than extreme poverty line.	No allowance made for higher costs in urban areas. Strong stress in the document on how rural poverty is much more serious; however, note is made that a significant proportion of the urban population live just above the poverty line, and that raising the poverty line by 10 percent would increase the incidence of urban poverty by over 20 percent.	World Bank (1999c)
Peru (1997)	Two poverty lines: the poverty line based on the food expenditure on food and non-food items by the population that spends exactly the value of the food poverty line on food; and the extreme poverty line, set at two-thirds of this.	Poverty line 1.66 times what the food poverty line would have been for Lima; 1.52, 1.66 and 1.68 for urban areas in Selva, Coast and Sierra.	Adjustments to poverty lines for rural and urban areas in three regions and for Lima, based on differences in the prices for food and non-food items.	World Bank (2002c)
Philippines (2000)	The proportion of people below the poverty line varied from 12 percent to 46 percent, depending on which of four poverty line criteria were used. Government statistics are based on access to a food basket providing 2,000 calories per person per day, plus a basket for non-food spending.	The World Bank and the government of the Philippines disagree on the poverty line; the Bank uses one that allows less funding for non-food spending (see page 4, box 1.1 footnote). No details given for how allowances for non-food needs are made.	Adjustment for different cost of food basket by region.	World Bank (2002a)
Sri Lanka (1995/96)	Two poverty lines: the lower poverty line based on the cost of food; and the upper poverty line, with some allowance for non-food needs.	The upper poverty line is 1.2 times that of the lower poverty line.	No allowance made for cost or price differences.	Sri Lanka, Government of (2002)
Swaziland (1995)	Two poverty lines: a food poverty line and a total poverty line (with some allowance for non-food needs). The food poverty line was based on cost of a food bundle that produced 2,100 calories per person per day. The food bundle was typical of the food consumption of the poorest 20 percent of households.	The total poverty line for urban areas was 1.51 times the food poverty line.	The total poverty line was slightly higher for urban areas than for rural areas, to allow for the higher cost of non-food items there (72.2 elamangeni compared to 67.25 elamangeni).	Swaziland, Kingdom of (1998)

Country (year)	Poverty line definition	Adjustment	Source
Tanzania (2000/01)	Two poverty lines: the food poverty line (minimum spending per person needed for 2,200 calories a day); and the basic needs poverty line (a small upward adjustment of the food poverty line for non-food needs). 'Basic needs' poverty line not based on the income needed to afford 'basic needs' but on the share of expenditure on non-food items of the poorest 25 percent of the population.	In 2000/01, the basic needs poverty line was 1.37 times the food poverty line.	Allowance made in both poverty lines for higher costs in Dar es Salaam (much the largest city) and 'other urban areas'.	Tanzania, United Republic of (2002a)
Togo (1987/89)	Two poverty lines: absolute poverty line based on cost of food; and poverty line with allowance for non-food needs.	Poverty line 1.67 times absolute poverty line for urban areas, 1.43 for small towns and 1.25 for rural areas.	Allowances made for differences in costs of non-food needs between urban, small town and rural areas.	World Bank (1996a)
Uruguay (1998)	Two poverty lines: indigent line based on food basket for protein and energy, with adjustments for higher costs in Montevideo; and poverty line with allowance for non-food needs, based on proportion of income spent on non-food items by second decile.	For Montevideo, poverty line was 3.1 times indigent line; for the rest of the population 2.75 times.	Allowances made for differences in costs of food and non-food needs between Montevideo and the rest of the nation.	World Bank (2001a)
Vietnam (1998)	Three different poverty lines in use: the food poverty line (average 2,100 kcal daily intake); the total poverty line; and a 'new' poverty line – with large variations in the scale of poverty depending on which of these is used.	The total poverty line was 1.39 times that of the food poverty line. The basis for the new poverty line is not clear.	Adjustments made to poverty lines, between island areas and rural mountainous areas, rural plain areas and urban areas.	Vietnam, Socialist Republic of (2002)
Yemen (1998)	Two poverty lines: a food poverty line, set to meet the needs represented by 2,200 calories per person; and an upper poverty line.	The upper poverty line is 1.52 times the food poverty line.	Both poverty lines adjusted between governorates and between rural and urban areas, although rural poverty lines were slightly higher than urban poverty lines.	Yemen, Republic of (2002)
Zambia (1998)	An overall poverty line and an extreme poverty line. The overall poverty line seems to be based only on the cost of a minimum food basket.	In 1998, the overall ('moderate') poverty line was 1.44 times the extreme poverty line (K 47,188 compared to K 32,861).	No mention made of any adjustments for spatial differences.	Zambia, Republic of (2002)
Zimbabwe (1995)	Lower poverty line based on cost of food; and upper poverty line, with allowance for other basic needs.	For urban areas, upper poverty line was 1.69 times that of the lower poverty line.	Upper urban poverty line 1.33 times that of the upper rural poverty line.	World Bank (1996b)

Annex 2: Levels of urban poverty

In most of the nations listed, there are two poverty lines: a food poverty line (often called the extreme poverty line), which is based only on the cost of a minimum food basket to satisfy calorific needs; and an absolute poverty line, where some allowance is made for non-food needs. Where two such poverty lines exist, the figures in this table are based on the absolute poverty line.

Furthermore, the figures below should not be compared between nations because of the (often very large) differences in the criteria used to set poverty lines.

Nation	Percentage of the urban population below the poverty line	Notes	Source
Bangladesh (1995)	60.9% (Dhaka 54.9%)	Based on 1.25 times the cost of food (for 2,112 kcals).	Islam et al (1997)
Bangladesh (2000)	36.6%	Based on the cost of food plus a small allowance for non-food items.	World Bank (2002b)
Bolivia (1996)	64.5%	Based on a poverty line that was twice the food poverty line.	Wodon (2000)
Brazil (1996)	29.2%	Based on a poverty line that was twice the food poverty line.	Wodon (2000)
Burkina Faso (1998)	16.5%	Seems to be based only on the cost of food.	Burkina Faso, Government of (2000)
Cambodia (1999)	Phnom Penh 14.6%; other urban 42.4%[85]	Based on a poverty line that was 1.42 times the food poverty line for Phnom Penh and 1.32 times the food poverty line for other urban.	Cambodia, Kingdom of (2002)
Cameroon (2001)	17.9% (10.9% for Douala; 13.3% for Yaounde)	Based on a poverty line that was 1.54 times the food poverty line.	Cameroon, Government of (2002)
Chad (1995/96)	35.0 (N'Djamena), 39.3 (other towns)	Based on a poverty line that was 1.33 the food poverty line for N'Djamena and 1.30 times for other towns.	Chad, Republic of (2003)
Chile (1996)	24.1%	Based on a poverty line that was twice the food poverty line.	Wodon (2000)
China (1998/99)	4.7%	Likely to be a considerable under-estimate as 100 million urban 'temporary migrants' not considered as 'urban'	GHK and IIED 2004
Colombia (1996)	52.2%	Based on a poverty line that was twice the food poverty line.	Wodon (2000)
Dominican Republic (1996)	29.3%	Based on a poverty line that was twice the food poverty line.	Wodon (2000)
Ethiopia (1995/96)	33% (varying from 72% in Dessie to 25% in Dire Dawa; for Addis Ababa it was 30%); rose to 37% in 1999/2000	Based on a total poverty line which was 1.78 times the food poverty line. and a 2,200 calorie intake for food.	World Bank (1999a)
Ecuador (1996)	55.2%	Based on a poverty line that was twice the food poverty line.	Wodon (2000)
Gambia (1998)	13.4% (Greater Banjul), 32.5% (other urban)	Based on an overall poverty line that was 1.66 times the food poverty line.	Gambia, the Republic of (2002)
Ghana (1998/99)	19.4% (3.8% in Accra)	1.29 times the extreme poverty line based only on the cost of food.	Ghana, Government of (2000)

---

[85] This is based on figures drawn from two rounds of the Cambodia Social and Economic Survey in 1999; note that significantly lower figures were given in the second round.

Guatemala (2000)	27.1%	2.26 times the extreme poverty line.	World Bank (2003a)
Honduras (1999)	57.3%	Based on 1.68 times the cost of a minimum food basket (the extreme poverty line).	World Bank (2001b)
Kenya (1997)	49%	Based on 2.1 times the food poverty line.	Kenya, Government of (2000)
Madagascar (1999)	52.1% (43.3% in urban Antananarivo)	Based on 1.21 times the food poverty line	Paternostro, Razafindravonona and Stifel (2001)
Malawi (1998)	54.9%	Based on 1.5 times the cost of food, and with allowances made for urban areas' higher expenditures on food (in part because of less self-production) and non-food items.	Malawi, Government of (2000)
Mauritania (1996)	26.8% (20.6% in Nouakchott; 37.8% in other cities)		Mauritania, Islamic Republic of (2000)
Mexico (1996)	20.5%	Based on a poverty line that was twice the food poverty line.	Wodon (2000)
Mongolia (1998)	39.4	Based on food poverty line plus what households whose income is around the cost of a minimum food basket spend on non food needs	Mearns 2004
Mozambique (1996/97)	62% (Maputo City 47.8%)	1.66 times the food poverty line.	Mozambique, Republic of (2001)
Nepal (1996/7)	23% (3.6% in Urban Kathmandu Valley, 34.3% other urban)	1.67 times the food poverty line	Prennushi 1999, Lanjouw, Prennushi and Zaidi 1999
Nicaragua (1998)	30.5% (Managua 18.5%)	1.9 times the extreme poverty line.	World Bank (2001c)
Niger (1993)	52% (Niamey 42%, other urban 58%)	1.5 times the extreme poverty line.	Niger, République du (2002)
Pakistan (1998/99)	23%		Pakistan, Government of the Islamic Republic of (2001)
Panama (1997)	15.3%	Based on full poverty line that was 1.74 times the extreme poverty line.	World Bank (1999c)
Paraguay (1996)	39.5%	Based on a poverty line that was twice the food poverty line.	Wodon (2000)
Peru (1997)	40.4% (varying from 34.1% for Lima to 52.8% for coast urban)	Allowance made for non-food items and for cost differences between rural and urban in different regions and for Lima.	World Bank (2002c)
Senegal (2001)	44-59% depending on the zone	Based on income level needed for food, but not clear if allowance was made for non-food needs.	Senegal, Republic of (2002)
Sri Lanka (1995/96)	25%	Upper poverty line based on 1.2 times the food poverty line.	Sri Lanka, Government of (2002)
Swaziland (1995)	45.2%	Total poverty line based on 1.51 times the food poverty line	Swaziland, Kingdom of (1998)

Tanzania, (2000/01)	17.6% for Dar es Salaam; 25.8% for other urban centres	Based on the 'basic needs' poverty line that was 1.37 times the food poverty line; urban poverty with regard to lack of basic services is much higher.	Tanzania, United Republic of (2002)
Togo (1987/89)	Between 12% and 30.5% depending on the urban centre	Based on 1.66 times the cost of food for urban centres and 1.43 for small towns.	World Bank (1996a)
Uruguay (1998)	24.7%	Based on 3.1 times the cost of food for Montevideo and 2.75 times the cost of food for other urban areas.	World Bank (2001a)
Venezuela (1996)	36.6%	Based on a poverty line that was twice the food poverty line.	Wodon (2000)
Vietnam (1998)	9%	Total poverty line.	Vietnam, Socialist Republic of (2002)
Yemen (1998)	30.8%	The upper poverty line based on 1.52 times the food poverty line.	Yemen, Republic of (2002)
Zambia (1998)	56.0%	Primarily on minimum food basket?	Zambia, Republic of (2002)

Annex 3: Infant and child mortality rates in rural and urban areas

Estimated mortality rates among infants (age less than 1) and children (ages 1-4)

| | Deaths per 1,000 births* | | | | | |
| | Age <1 | | | Age 1-4 | | |
Country and Year	Urban	Rural	Total	Urban	Rural	Total
SUB-SAHARAN AFRICA						
Benin (1996)	84	112	104	72	98	90
Burkina Faso (1998/99)	67	113	109	66	137	130
Cameroon (1998)	61	87	80	53	80	72
Central African Rep. (1994/95)	80	116	102	53	70	63
Chad (1997)	99	113	110	101	103	103
Comoros (1996)	64	90	84	18	36	32
Côte d'Ivoire (1994)	75	100	91	49	73	65
Eritrea (1995)	80	74	76	53	92	83
Ethiopia (2000)	97	115	113	58	88	85
Gabon (2000)	61	62	61	30	40	32
Ghana (1998)	43	68	61	36	58	52
Guinea (1999)	79	116	107	76	107	99
Kenya (1998)	55	74	71	35	38	37
Madagascar (1997)	78	105	99	53	77	72
Malawi (2000)	83	117	113	71	106	102
Mali (1996)	99	145	134	102	149	137
Mozambique (1997)	101	160	147	55	92	84
Namibia (1992)	63	61	62	25	36	32
Niger (1998)	80	147	136	107	212	193
Nigeria (1999)	59	75	71	52	73	67
Rwanda (1992)	88	90	90	74	80	80
Senegal (1997)	50	79	69	41	94	75
Sudan (1990)	74	79	77	46	71	63
Tanzania (1996)	82	97	94	42	59	56
Togo (1998)	65	85	80	38	79	69
Uganda (1995)	74	88	86	64	78	77
Zambia (1996)	92	118	108	90	98	95
Zimbabwe (1999)	47	65	60	23	37	33
NEAR EAST & NORTH AFRICA						
Egypt (2000)	43	62	55	10	19	15
Jordan (1997)	27	39	29	5	7	5
Morocco (1992)	52	69	63	7	31	22
Turkey (1998)	42	59	48	10	16	12
Yemen (1997)	75	94	90	22	38	35
EUROPE & EURASIA						
Kazakhstan (1999)	44	64	55	7	10	9
Kyrgyz Republic (1997)	54	70	66	4	13	10
Uzbekistan (1996)	43	44	44	9	14	12

ASIA & PACIFIC

Bangladesh (2000)	74	81	80	24	35	33
Cambodia (2000)	72	96	93	22	34	32
India (1999)	49	80	73	17	35	31
Indonesia (1997)	36	58	52	12	22	19
Nepal (1996)	61	95	93	23	53	51
Pakistan (1990/91)	75	102	94	21	33	29
Philippines (1998)	31	40	36	15	23	20
Vietnam (1997)	23	37	35	7	12	12

LATIN AMERICA & CARIBBEAN

Bolivia (1998)	53	100	74	20	38	28
Brazil (1996)	42	65	48	7	15	9
Colombia (2000)	21	31	24	3	5	4
Dominican Republic (1996)	46	53	49	9	18	13
Guatemala (1998/99)	49	49	49	9	20	16
Haiti (2000)	87	91	89	27	65	53
Nicaragua (1997)	40	51	45	9	14	11
Paraguay (1990)	33	39	36	13	10	11
Peru (2000)	28	60	43	11	27	18

*Infant and child mortality rates for the 10-year period preceding the survey.
Source: Demographic and Health Surveys {Demographic and Health Surveys (DHS), 2002, #39}.

Annex 4: IIED Publications on urban poverty and on other urban issues

a. The Working Papers series on poverty

Alimuddin, Salim, Arif Hasan and Asiya Sadiq (2001*), Community-driven Water and Sanitation: The Work of the Anjuman Samaji Behbood and the Larger Faisalabad Context*, Working Paper 7. IIED, London.

Baumann, Ted, Joel Bolnick and Diana Mitlin (2002), *The Age of Cities and Organizations of the Urban Poor: The Work of the South African Homeless People's Federation and the People's Dialogue on Land and Shelter*, Working Paper 2. IIED, London.

Boonyabancha, Somsook (2003), *A Decade of Change: from the Urban Community Development Office (UCDO) to the Community Organizations Development Institute (CODI) in Thailand. Increasing Community Options through a National Government Development Programme*, Working Paper 12. IIED, London

Cain, Allan, Mary Daly and Paul Robson (2002), *Basic Service Provision for the Urban Poor; The Experience of Development Workshop in Angola*, Working Paper 8. IIED, London.

Dávila, Julio D (2001), *Urban Poverty Reduction Experiences in Cali, Colombia: Lessons from the Work of Local Non-profit Organizations*, Working Paper 4. IIED, London.

Díaz, Andrés Cabanas, Emma Grant, Paula Irene del Cid Vargas and Verónica Sajbin Velásquez (2001), *El Mezquital - A Community's Struggle for Development*, Working Paper 1. IIED, London.

Mitlin, Diana (2004) *Understanding Urban Poverty; What the Poverty Reduction Strategy Papers tell us*, Working Paper 13. IIED, London

Patel, Sheela and Diana Mitlin (2002), *The Work of SPARC and its Partners Mahila Milan and the National Slum Dwellers Federation in India*, Working Paper 5. IIED, London.

Schusterman, Ricardo, Florencia Almansi, Ana Hardoy, Cecilia Monti and Gastón Urquiza (2002), *Poverty Reduction in Action: Participatory Planning in San Fernando, Buenos Aires*, Working Paper 6. IIED, London.

Stein, Alfredo (2001), *Participation and Sustainability in Social Projects: The Experience of the Local Development Programme (PRODEL) in Nicaragua*, Working Paper 3. IIED, London.

Satterthwaite, David (2002), *Reducing Urban Poverty: Some Lessons From Experience*, Working Paper 11. IIED, London.

Satterthwaite, David (2004), *The Under-estimation of Urban Poverty in Low and Middle-income Nations*, Working paper 14. IIED, London.

HOW TO OBTAIN THESE: Printed versions can be obtained from http://www.earthprint.com/ for US$ 9 each plus postage and packing (for the UK, US$ 5 for first item, US$ 2.50 for additional items; for Europe, US$ 6 for first item, US$ 3 for additional items; for elsewhere, US$ 10 for first item, US$ 5 for additional items). Electronic versions may be obtained at no charge from IIED's web-page: http://www.iied.org/urban/downloads.html. If you have any difficulties obtaining these, e-mail us on humans@iied.org with details as to which working paper you want.

b. Other publications from this research programme

Shorter versions of the working papers on PRODEL and on El Mezquital have been published in IIED's journal *Environment and Urbanization*:

Stein, Alfredo (2001), "Participation and sustainability in social projects: the experience of the Local Development Programme (PRODEL) in Nicaragua", *Environment and Urbanization* Vol 13 No 1, pages 11-35.

Díaz, Andrés Cabanas, Emma Grant, Paula Irene del Cid Vargas and Verónica Sajbin Velásquez (2001), "The role of external agencies in the development of El Mezquital in Guatemala City", *Environment and Urbanization* Vol 13, No 1, pages 91-100.

Díaz, Andrés Cabanas, Emma Grant, Paula Irene del Cid Vargas and Verónica Sajbin Velásquez (2000), "El Mezquital - a community's struggle for development in Guatemala City", *Environment and Urbanization* Vol 12, No 1, pages 87-106.

HOW TO OBTAIN THESE: These papers may be obtained electronically from the web at www.ingentaselect.com; http://www.ingentaselect.com/titles/09562478.htm takes you straight to *Environment and Urbanization* On-line. Access to these papers is free.

c. Other publications on urban poverty

Mitlin, Diana and David Satterthwaite (editors), *Empowering Squatter Citizen: Local Government, Civil Society and Urban Poverty Reduction*, Earthscan Publications, London, April 2004. This can be obtained from book stores or from www.earthscan.co.uk.

Civil Society in Action: Transforming Opportunities for the Urban Poor: The October 2001 issue of *Environment and Urbanization* was prepared with Shack Dwellers International (SDI), a network of community organizations in Africa, Asia and Latin America. It includes articles by members on strategies and approaches that have been found to be of particular importance - for example; the use of savings and credit as a means of building strong local organizations, and an illustration of how the process has taken hold in a number of new countries. It also includes perspectives from a range of development professionals and agencies on the significance of SDI and a description of new relations with local authorities and state agencies that the grassroots organizations have been able to negotiate. Photo-essays on community site development and construction show some of the work of urban poor federations in the Philippines and Cambodia.

Rethinking Aid to Urban Poverty Reduction: Lessons for Donors: The April 2001 issue of *Environment and Urbanization* includes evaluations of urban projects or programmes funded by US AID, the World Bank, DFID, Sida, NORAD and UNICEF, along with papers considering the constraints on donor effectiveness. There are also papers on participatory budgeting in Brazil, a fund for community initiatives in Uganda, poverty-mapping in Argentina, mapping infrastructure deficiencies in Salvador (Brazil), community-based watershed management, and links between poverty and transport.

Poverty Reduction and Urban Governance: The April 2000 issue of *Environment and Urbanization* includes 12 papers which examine the links between poverty and governance in particular cities. Among the interesting points of commonality or contrast are: the great range of political structures, with some cities having governments that are clearly more accountable and responsive to urban poor groups than others; the very limited powers, resources and capacities available to urban governments to raise revenues; the complex political economies within all the cities that influence who gets land for housing, infrastructure and services; and the capacity of anti-poor local government policies and practices to harm the livelihoods of many low-income groups within their jurisdiction.

The two issues of *Environment and Urbanization* planned for 2005 are on poverty-related themes: Improving the Lives of Slum Dwellers *(*April 2005) and Chronic Poverty (October 2005).

HOW TO OBTAIN THESE: The printed versions of each issue of *Environment and Urbanization* can be obtained from http://www.earthprint.com/ for US$18 plus postage and packing (for the UK, US$ 5 for first item, US$ 2.50 for additional items; for Europe, US$ 6 for first item, US$ 3 for additional items; for elsewhere, US$ 10 for first item, US$ 5 for additional items).

The full text of these issues can be accessed at www.ingentaselect.com; http://www.ingentaselect.com/titles/09562478.htm takes you straight to *Environment&Urbanization* On-line. Access to these is free, except for the three most recent issues (where access to each paper costs US$ 6).

d. Urban publications with Earthscan

McGranahan, Gordon and Frank Murray (editors) (2003), *Air Pollution and Health in Rapidly Developing Countries*, Earthscan Publications, London, 227 pages.

McGranahan, Gordon, Pedro Jacobi, Jacob Songsore, Charles Surjadi and Marianne Kjellén (2001), *The Citizens at Risk: From Urban Sanitation to Sustainable Cities*, Earthscan Publications, London, 200 pages.

Hardoy, Jorge E, Diana Mitlin and David Satterthwaite (2001), *Environmental Problems in an Urbanizing World: Finding Solutions for Cities in Africa, Asia and Latin America*, Earthscan Publications, London, 470 pages.

Bartlett, Sheridan, Roger Hart, David Satterthwaite, Ximena de la Barra and Alfredo Missair (1999), *Cities for Children: Children's Rights, Poverty and Urban Management*, Earthscan, London, 305 pages.

Satterthwaite, David (editor) (1999), *The Earthscan Reader in Sustainable Cities*, Earthscan Publications, London, 472 pages.

Satterthwaite, David, Roger Hart, Caren Levy, Diana Mitlin, David Ross, Jac Smit and Carolyn Stephens (1996), *The Environment for Children*, Earthscan Publications and UNICEF, London and New York, 284 pages.

Hardoy, Jorge E and David Satterthwaite (1989), *Squatter Citizen: Life in the Urban Third World*, Earthscan Publications, London, UK, 388 pages.

HOW TO OBTAIN THESE: These are available from Earthscan Publications, 8-12 Camden High Street, London NW1 0JH, UK, e-mail: earthinfo@earthscan.co.uk; web: www.earthscan.co.uk. Also available in bookstores. Earthscan books are available in the USA from Stylus, 22883 Quicksilver Drive, Sterling, VA 20166-2012, USA, e-mail: styluspub@aol.com. In Canada, Earthscan books are available from Renouf Publishing Company, 1- 5369 Canotek Road, Ottawa, Ontario K1J 9J3, Canada, e-mail: orderdept@renoufbooks.com. The Earthscan web site also has details of Earthscan representatives and agents in all other countries.

e. Other Working Papers series

There are two other Working Papers series in addition to the series on Poverty Reduction in Urban Areas:
1. Working Papers on Rural Urban Interactions and Livelihood Strategies, which include case studies from Tanzania, Mali and Nigeria.
2. Working Papers on Urban Environmental Action Plans and Local Agenda 21s, with case studies from Colombia, Ghana, Indonesia, Malaysia, Namibia, Peru, Senegal, South Africa, Uganda and the UK.

HOW TO OBTAIN THESE: Printed versions can be obtained from http://www.earthprint.com/ for US$ 9 each plus postage and packing (for the UK, US$ 5 for first item, US$ 2.50 for additional items; for Europe, US$ 6 for first item, US$ 3 for additional items; for elsewhere, US$10 for first item, US$ 5 for additional items).

Electronic versions may be obtained at no charge from IIED's web-page: http://www.iied.org/urban/downloads.html. If you have any difficulties obtaining these, e-mail us on humans@iied.org with details as to which working paper you want.

f. Other IIED publications on urban issues

Environment and Urbanization: Now in its 16th year, this is one of the most cited and widely distributed international journals on urban issues. Each issue has a special theme and includes: 9-14 papers on that theme; a guide to the literature on the theme and profiles of innovative NGOs (in some issues) and Book Notes (summaries of new books, research reports and newsletters, and how these can be obtained (including those in Spanish, French and Portuguese).

Frequency:	Twice yearly (April and October of each year)
Volume numbers:	Volume 15 (2003), Volume 16 (2004), Volume 17 (2005)
Subscription prices:	One year: institutions - £78 or US$ 130; individuals £28 or US$ 47 Two year: institutions - £132 or US$ 220; individuals £48 or US$ 80 Three year: institutions - £192 or US$ 320; individuals £68 or US$ 113

Half-price subscriptions available to subscribers from Latin America, Asia (except Japan, Singapore and Hong Kong) and Africa, and to students (xerox of current student card needed as proof).

Postage for subscriptions: The above prices include air mail post; subscriptions can start at any point in the year.

World Wide Web: The contents page of the latest issue and the summaries of all papers in French, Spanish and English, the editorial and the Book Notes Section are on http://www.iied.org/eandu/. This site also includes details of subscription prices and the price of back issues.

Environment and Urbanization On-line: The full text of the current issue and many back issues are available on the web at http://www.ingentaselect.com/titles/09562478.htm. All issues published from 1995 to the present, except for the three most recent issues, are available free. Institutional subscribers get free access to all on-line issues; to do so, they must register at www.ingentaselect.com.